Motor Mania

TopGear

Motor Mania

Ivan Berg and Nik Berg

BBC
BOOKS

First published 2006

6 8 10 9 7 5

Copyright © Ivan Berg and Nik Berg 2006

The moral right of the authors has been asserted.

ISBN-13: 978 0 563 49362 4

ISBN-10: 0 563 49362 3

Published by BBC Books, BBC Worldwide Ltd, Woodlands,
80 Wood Lane, London W12 0TT

Commissioning editor: Shirley Patton
Project editor: Christopher Tinker
Copy-editor: Helen Armitage
Designer: Jo Ridgeway
Cover design: Owen Norris
Picture researcher: Giles Chapman
Production controller: Peter Hunt

Set in ITC Officina and Aachen by BBC Books
Printed and bound in Italy by L.E.G.O. SpA
Origination by Dot Gradations, Wickford, Essex

Page 2: The flying ConvAircar (see page 173)

Contents

Introduction **7**

One: Life in the Fast Lane **9**
Eating, sleeping, shagging – you know, all the stuff people
do in their cars when they're not actually driving

Two: 'Any Color, So Long As It's Black' **26**
History is bunk. And we do like a bit of bunk

Three: Motorworld **41**
The driving habits of Johnny Foreigner

Four: Pop Idle **83**
Geddit? Motor music, maestro, please

Five: Screen Machines **98**
Stars in cars, cars as stars. Even the odd OsCAR

Six: Police! Stop! **119**
Speeding and thieving. Look out for the flashing blue lights

Seven: Wacky Racers **134**
The fast and the furious ... from Formula None to Formula One

Eight: 'Vorsprung durch Technik' **147**
How to get ahead in advertising – or not

Nine: Beetlemania

The cult cars we fell in love with

159

Ten: Flying Cars and Superhighways

Forwards and back to the future of motoring

171

Picture Credits

191

The Authors

192

Introduction

This book will not help you choose your next car. It won't help you fix your current one either. It's not an encyclopaedia. In fact it's of very little practical value at all. Instead it's distracting, diverting, amusing, annoying, entertaining and unforgettable.

Inside you'll find the first traffic jam caused by jam, the only nude car show and the best car to attend it in (the Daihatsu Naked), the best ways to cook roadkill and the Bumper Dumper you'll inevitably need afterwards. You'll meet the man who made an orchestra from an Accord, the worst Formula One drivers, the African dictator-turned-car-designer and the drugs baron with a car addiction. We've got flying cars, clockwork cars, atomic cars and 2CVs turned into speedboats. Enough facts, stats and stories to fill your trivia tank.

If this book were a car it'd be a Mazda MX-5 – small, completely impractical, but big fun – and until it came along nobody knew they wanted it.

ONE

Life in the Fast Lane

What do you do in your car? Apart from drive it, that is. Bet you've had a bite to eat, a drink, a nap. It's more than likely that you have had sex, or tried to have sex in your car, maybe even conceived your first born. We live in our cars, pray in them, get married in them, shop in them, do our banking in them, are entertained in them and work in them. Eventually, we even get driven to our graves in them. This chapter, then, is all about everything except actually driving the things.

Love and Marriage in your Carriage

From car-park crumpet to wedded bliss, the car is the ultimate sex machine.

Carma Sutra

Amorous couples in Vinci, Italy, can head for the world's first Love Car Park. Screened from prying eyes by high hedges and boasting romantic soft lighting, the car park gives young couples somewhere to car-noodle in peace. Nine out of ten Italians live with their parents until well into their twenties, so back-seat bonking is extremely common. According to one of Italy's regular summer sex surveys, 88 per cent of Italians claimed to have had at least one sexual encounter in a car. Which probably accounts for the phenomenal success of the original Fiat Panda – its seats converted easily into a double bed.

Chinese Whispers

There's been a surge of in-car sex in China due to the recent huge increase in car ownership. Like the Italians, the Chinese also live with their parents until either work or marriage provides an escape route. The problem with frisky couples in cars became acute in 2003 in the city of Guangzhou. The Xinhua news agency reported that the city's Mt Baiyunshan Park was the focus for the evening in-car activities. The report said that the police could only request couples to leave the park as it was not clear whether they were committing an offence. A lawyer from the city, one Gan Mingyong, suggested that 'a private car provides a specific private space for its owner to exercise his or her own human rights.'

Bench Marque

The 200mph Vector supercar was supposed to be America's answer to Ferrari and Lamborghini and employed aerospace technology in its construction. What made it even more unusual was its bench seat – specifically designed so that driver and passenger could get 'up close and personal'.

Hitching a Ride

Las Vegas, Nevada, is home to several drive-thru wedding chapels. At A Little White Wedding Chapel (actually tried and tested by Berg Jr and Mrs Berg Jr – sadly, sans Cadillac) the service costs just $55 if you have your own car. Bride and groom drive through the 'Tunnel of Vows' complete with a romantic ceiling decorated with cherubs and starlights. Although it's a speedy service it has been known to last longer than some marriages. Despite rumours to the contrary, there's no drive-thru divorce court yet.

A Caddy, the King and a drive-thru wedding ceremony. Only in Las Vegas.
Thankyouverymuch.

Drive-in, Strip-off

Unmarried (or even unhappily married) gentlemen might like to know that The Climax Gentleman's Club just outside Pittsburgh, Pennsylvania, is the world's only drive-thru strip club. It looks a bit like a car wash, but the only waxing in evidence is on the girls posing for your pleasure. And those feeling guilty about a visit can always repent at a drive-thru church. There are auto-friendly churches in Daytona Beach, Florida, and in Tucson, Arizona.

Born to Drive

In-car sex can sometimes lead to an in-car birth and there's nothing like being born behind the wheel to get you off to a racing start in life.

Speedy Deliveries

A 2005 TV campaign by the UK's Automobile Association claimed that AA Patrolmen helped to deliver 18 babies in 2004. So do AA men carry hot towels alongside their socket sets and jump leads? Not exactly. They 'helped' by rescuing women in labour from conked-out cars and delivering them to hospital where the babies were born.

To the Minor Born

We could find no statistics on the number of babies actually born in a car. But we can name three of them, all born in 2005. Dylan Fawcett, delivered in a North Yorkshire blizzard on the A64 in the family Ford Fiesta in the early hours of Tuesday, 23 February 2005. Aliyah Elizabeth Pacheco, born in her parents' Renault Mégane in Ealing, west London, with the help of police constable Mark Tabran on Saturday, 2 April 2005, also in the early hours.

Delivery number three is noteworthy because it was caught on camera by a Kansas City, Missouri, KCTV5 news crew who just happened to be passing. Jay Mance was born at 8.56 a.m. in the front seat of his dad's car on the hard shoulder of Kansas Interstate 35 on the morning of Tuesday, 3 May 2005.

A Life on the Open Road

You're never homeless with a Honda, Hyundai, or Hummer.

A Hardtop over your Head

Thousands of people live their lives on the road. In Canada, it's reckoned that four out of five homeless people live in their automobiles. A car provides a roof over your head, heating in winter and a view that changes every day (as long as you have money for gas). Eugene, Oregon, even has a number of designated car campsites. And if you do live in your car, you'll be in good company. Oscar-winning actress Hilary Swank and comedians David Letterman and Jim Carrey have all spent time living in their cars before hitting the big time.

Need to Go on the Go?

There's no need to get out of the car if you're caught short on the freeway in the USA, provided that you have invested in a 'Little John' portable urinal. Simply unzip and let rip into this specially sculpted container – you don't even need to stand. You'll be reassured to learn that it's made from unbreakable plastic and has a spill-proof cap. Ladies? No problem. 'Little John' has a companion urinary director (*sic*) 'Lady Jane' female adapter. For extra spillage protection a locking zip pouch is included in the price. If it's something more substantial that needs to be, er, exhausted, you can buy one of Uncle Booger's original 'Bumper Dumpers'. This patented device can be clipped to a vehicle's tow-bar or used as a stand-alone unit. It's got a full-size portable toilet seat. Receptacles can be buckets or plastic bags, depending on user choice.

Micro and Macro Motor-Homes

Of course, if you drive a motor-home, you'll have no need of 'Little-Johns' or 'Bumper Dumpers' because you'll have your very own private lavatory. Mind you, it'd be a bit of a squeeze in the world's smallest motor-home, the 10-foot-6-inch-long Daihatsu Hijetta. This two-berth conversion of the Daihatsu Jetta microbus, by specialist converter East Sussex UK-based outfit JC Leisure, not only boasts two beds but also a two-burner gas hob, kitchen sink, an auxiliary battery and a 'Porta-Potti' portable lavatory.

Nearly four Hijettas can be parked in the space taken up by what is probably the world's most fantastical motor-home, the Winnebago Vectra. This air-conditioned luxury mansion on wheels starred in the movies *About Schmidt* and *Meet the Fockers*. It has a double bedroom with king-size bed, six-seat dining area, six-seat lounge with bar, electric fireplace and multi-media entertainment centre with 30-inch flat-screen TV, full-size shower and toilet room and a fully equipped kitchen. Motive power is provided by a 400hp diesel. The Hijetta makes do with 64bhp.

The Bare Necessities

While you're saving up for a motor-home here are a few recommended accessories for in-car living:

1. *Solar shower – solar-heated self-contained shower bag and shower head you can hang on the branch of a tree.*

2. *Restop I and Restop II – 'personal lavatory pouches' that contain absorbent crystals that turn number ones and number twos into*

The Winnebago Vectra is a mobile mansion with a bedroom, bar, dining room and even a fireplace. Driven by wealthy Fockers.

inoffensive gel. Each pouch has a built-in funnel to make aiming easier. The Restop II has been designed to line a special Commode Bucket, complete with padded foam seat.

3. *Sure-Pak MREs – pack of 12 Meals Ready-to-Eat in long-life sealed-foil pouches. All come with an entrée, side dish, dessert, crackers, cracker spread, beverage powder, spoon and towelette.*

4. *Disposable underwear – men's and women's sizes in packs of five.*

5. *Space Brand survival blanket – metalized silver and gold reflective blanket invented for NASA. Weighs 2 oz and fits in the palm of your hand.*

6. *12-volt electric blanket – plugs into cigar lighter, warms to 75°F (24°C) and draws just 4 amps. And also plugging into the cigar lighter: a hair curler, a hair dryer and a drink-heating element.*

7. *Emergency jump starter/power supply – to use when all the 12-volt gear drains your battery.*

Fast Food

Whether it's a hit-and-run or a drive-thru there's always plenty to eat on the road.

Naked Lunch

It's hungry work driving. Fortunately, there are 30,000 McDonald's restaurants in the world, and more than 12,000 of those have drive-thru windows so you can snack without even stopping. The famous Golden Arches opened their first drive-thru in 1948, but the dubious honour of being the first restaurant to offer 'curb service' goes to The Pig Stand in Dallas, Texas, which opened in 1921, serving its famous 'Pig Sandwich', onion rings and 'Texas Toast'.

The Varsity in Atlanta, Georgia, claims to be the world's biggest drive-in restaurant with a capacity of 600 cars. Founded in 1928, The Varsity's specialities are chilli fries and hot dogs, served 'naked' (plain on a bun) or 'red' (ketchup) or 'yellow' (mustard). The Varsity can host 800 customers at any one time and on a busy day claims to serve an astonishing 30,000 people.

Roadkill Recipes

Don't try to dodge that deer – it could be lunch. If you're smart you can be self-sufficient when it comes to food on the move. Most of the mammals that get mashed on the road can be scooped up and served on a plate. And, as long as you haven't squashed the poor creature yourself, in most countries it's perfectly legal. Here are a few ideas to get your gastric juices going.

Pheasant Loaf

Ingredients
2 pheasants
¾ lb pork
a good handful of hazelnuts, pine kernels and pistachios
½ pint single cream
salt and pepper to taste
1 teaspoon olive oil
10 slices parma ham

Method
Don't worry if the pheasant is in a mess – you'll need to remove the meat from the bones anyway and chop, though not too finely. Chop the pork in a similar fashion and put all the meat in a bowl. Add the nuts, cream and seasoning and mix well. Spread oil on a large sheet of foil, then lay the parma ham on top, overlapping the slices. Place the nutty pheasant and pork mixture in the middle and wrap the ham around it. Massage the loaf until it is 3–4 inches thick. Wrap the foil tightly around it and bake in the oven at 350°F/180°C for 40 minutes.

Baked Hedgehog (or Porcupine)

Ingredients
1 hedgehog (or porcupine)
wet clay

Method
Clean the hedgehog or porcupine by soaking in water and then gut it – you'll probably have to do this yourself, as no self-respecting butcher is

likely to touch it, so mind the prickles! Wrap it in the clay, making sure all the spines are covered. Cook in a medium oven for two hours. When the clay has hardened, break it open and the spines should come with it.

Kangaroo Roast

Ingredients

For the marinade
olive oil
375 ml red wine
3 cloves
3 bay leaves
6 juniper berries
black pepper to taste
4 kangaroo fillets (allow ½ lb per person)

For the sauce
2 chopped carrots
3 chopped celery sticks
3 chopped onions
olive oil
6 rashers streaky bacon
1½ pints meat stock

Method
Make a marinade with the olive oil, wine, cloves, bay leaves, juniper berries and black pepper. Marinade the kangaroo fillets overnight. For the sauce, sautée all the vegetables in olive oil, then add the bacon. Deglaze the pan (by adding the strained marinade to loosen the stuck bits of veg) and reduce by three-quarters. Add the stock and simmer until the sauce is thick. Meanwhile, fry the fillets over a high heat to seal them, then place them in a hot oven (480°F/250°C) for five minutes. Rest them for a few minutes before serving with the sauce.

Crankcase Cuisine

If you can't wait to get your ill-gotten game in the oven, then you could cook it on the way home instead. Engine temperatures are just right for a nice slow-cook. In their book *Manifold Destiny*, Americans Chris Maynard and Bill Scheller detail how to create mouth-watering masterpieces as you drive, with cooking times measured in miles, not minutes. Wrapping your food in layers of foil, pressing it on the hottest part of the engine and heading down the highway, slowly cooks the food to perfection.

Tow-bar Barbie

If you have time to stop and cook and prefer your meat burnt and smoky – and you have a tow- or hitch-bar – then you can clamp on the Blue Ridge Mountain twin-burner gas-powered portable barbecue. Made in the Blue Ridge Mountains in southcentral Pennsylvania, this 24×16-inch grill will cater for a minibus-full of outdoor-eating fans. Make sure the vehicle's petrol-tank filler-cap is tight on – otherwise you might inadvertently barbecue more than you bargained for.

Road Works

Change the view from your office window and take your work with you.

In-car Internet

It's the 21st century, so of course lots of executive cars come equipped with heavyweight communications systems that can download your SMS messages and e-mails as you drive. But it's not the same as having a proper PC – for a start you can't see all the hilarious videos and photos your colleagues are e-mailing you. So for the full car–office experience you'll need an in-car PC. We like the Datenblatt InDash CarPC as it slots into the space where your stereo normally goes and has a DVD-drive and 40GB hard drive.

Dashboard Desk

A dashboard is no substitute for a desk, but fortunately a number of companies make devices to hold your laptop securely in your car. Our favourite, though, is the Wheel Mate steering-wheel desk, which clamps over your car's steering wheel to provide a non-slip working surface. It even has a cup holder. Of course, you'll have to park before you use it or all your paperwork will go flying at the first corner.

Carfee Break

No office is complete without a coffee machine. There are plenty of 12-volt powered percolators to be found, but among the most stylish is the Velox Coffeebreak Car. Made of heavy-duty ABS plastic, it's designed by Bertone who brought us the Maserati Khamsin, Lancia Stratos, Lamborghini Countach and … the Daewoo Espero. Well, no-one's perfect – but the coffee is dispensed at an ideal 180°F (82°C).

Driving Can Seriously Damage your Health

Never mind crashing, just sitting in your car can be a major health hazard.

The Toxic Avenger

That 'new-car smell' you get as you drive away from the showroom could make you seriously sick. The cocktail of chemicals released from glues, paints, vinyls and plastics inside your new car can cause headaches, drowsiness and other problems, say researchers in Australia. Among the nasties released are benzene, acetone and toluene, according to a two-year study by Australia's Commonwealth Scientific and Industrial Research Organisation (CSIRO). Citroën's 2005 model-year C4 made a virtue of the smelly car – it came with vials of perfume that get gently filtered through the ventilation system to make the car smell sweet. Flavours include 'Fleur de Lotus' and 'Cannelle Gingembre'. Yum.

Beetles, Bugs and Bacteria

The average car is teeming with more germs and moulds than a toilet seat, according to researchers. More than 500 colonies of bacteria, including *Staphylococcus* and *Bacillus* were found by microbiologists who conducted a survey for car-care company Comma. Not surprisingly, dog owners have the dirtiest cars, followed by single men and then single women. Family cars, despite the prospect of baby drool and nappy mishaps, were next, with mature motorists boasting the cleanest cars. The dirtiest parts of the car were found to be the steering wheel (a festering ground for *Staphylococcus* – most commonly associated with nose-picking) and the boot and footwell, which harbour plenty of *Bacillus*, normally found in soil and stagnant water. Better get that vac out then – or make sure you buy your next used car from an oldie.

Life Support

You might not fancy eating the seats, but your car can keep you alive in an emergency, as 88-year-old Mary Lillian Anderson of Vancouver, Washington, proved in January 2006. She went off the road in her 1997 Cadillac Seville and was trapped for six days before being rescued. As if that weren't enough, all of the car's king-size cup holders were empty, so Anderson survived by wiping condensation off the windows with a towel and sucking out the moisture.

The End of the Road

One day, we'll all be driven into the ground.

Drive-thru, Check-out

From food and drink to pharmaceuticals, pretty much everything you need in life can be obtained at an American drive-thru. Everything in death, too. The G. W. Thompson Chapel of Remembrance in Spartanburg, South Carolina, has a drive-thru funeral service. The deceased's coffin remains on display in a special window, while mourners drive by to pay their respects. Apparently, it's very popular, with more than a third of customers going for the drive-thru.

Buried in a Benz

In Teshi, a village about 10 miles east of Accra in Ghana, wood-carving craftsmen specialize in making coffins in the shape of a Mercedes-Benz. The more realistic the car, the more the coffin costs. Customers who can afford them order early and put them on display until required.

Monumental Parking Meters

Two parking meters are incorporated in plumber Archie Arnold's tombstone in Scipio Cemetery, Harlan, Indiana. Archie accidentally damaged both while on a visit to Hicksville, Ohio, and had to pay for their replacement. The local sheriff let him keep them, and Archie, knowing he was dying from liver disease, modified his will to state that upon his death the parking meters were to be placed on each end of his tombstone and that they were to read 'EXPIRED'. The coin slots are welded shut – presumably to prevent pranksters paying for extra time.

Afterlife in the Fast Lane

It's not just Rolls-Royce that has a Phantom, you know.

Dean's Death and the Cursed Car

The demise of Hollywood heart-throb James Dean behind the wheel of his Porsche Speedster on 30 September 1955 wasn't the end of the carnage caused by this mysterious motor. In fact, it was just the beginning for 'The Little Bastard', as the car was nicknamed. Shortly after Dean died, legendary car customizer George Barris bought the wreck. When it was delivered to his garage, it fell on one of his mechanics, breaking both his legs. Barris sold parts from the car to two doctors racing at the Pomona Fair Grounds, Los Angeles, on 24 October 1956. Both crashed. The first, Troy McHenry, died when his car hit a tree and the second,

James Dean's 'The Little Bastard' certainly lived up to its name. It killed Dean and two others, sparked a huge blaze and then disappeared.

William Eschrid, survived a huge crash, despite sustaining multiple injuries. Two of the Porsche's tyres were sold to a young man and he narrowly avoided a huge crash when both blew simultaneously. Barris then loaned the wreck to the California Highway Patrol who planned to use it in a road-safety exhibit, but the garage storing the Speedster burned to the ground. Every car in it was destroyed – except The Little Bastard. While on display in Sacramento the car fell from its display, breaking the hip of a teenager, and, as its final gesture, the Speedster fell on George Barkus, the driver transporting it to its road-safety expo, killing him. The cursed car mysteriously disappeared in 1960 *en route* from Miami, Florida, to Los Angeles, California, and has not been heard of since.

Ride a Haunted Hearse

If anything is going to be haunted, you'd expect it to be a hearse. There must be more than a few souls who enjoyed the last ride so much that they decided to hang around. Destiny Tours of Sydney, Australia, has turned that idea into a thriving tourist business, using plush 1967 Cadillac LaSalle hearses. We can do no better than quote their blurb:

Are you brave enough to ride with the Hearse Whisperer and Elvira or Morticia, the haunted hearses? Are you a skeptic or non-believer in ghosts? There is no need to walk around dark and dusty old buildings with a Weird Sydney Ghost and History Tour. We have our own regular spirits accompanying us in the hearses! Come along on a Weird Sydney Ghost and History Tour and see for yourself!

Very important: *Please note that Destiny Tours Sydney encourages respect for the deceased and the spirits that come and go in our vehicles. Do the tour and don't forget your camera. However, often cameras do not work in and around the cars, and many times photos of the cars turn out with unexplainable anomalies in them.*

Sydney Psychic and Medium June Cleeland rides the hearses regularly to charge her psychic batteries and says:

Spirits clamour to the cars because many thousands of corpses were carried to their final resting place and a lot of emotion surrounds each vehicle. Hauntings are brought about by this and also because the spirits sense the fear and excitement of the passengers, and of course the passengers are also opening up their senses to the unknown which makes them more susceptible to sightings and feelings etc.

TWO

'Any Color, So Long As It's Black'

Henry Ford once famously said that 'History is more or less bunk ... the only history that matters a tinker's damn is the history we made today.' The bunk in this chapter is mostly about automobile 'firsts' – including Henry's own unique contribution to its history.

Left Behind

Rut marks on the old Roman road surface at an archaeological dig in Britain suggested that the Romans drove their chariots on the left. Otherwise there appears to be little factual evidence as to why the British and around a quarter of the world's population drive on the left and the rest drive on the right. It's almost certainly due to the fact that most people are right-handed. Jousting knights with their lances under their right arm naturally passed on each other's right and if you passed a stranger on the road you walked on the left to keep your sword arm between yourself and a potential assailant. Napoleon Bonaparte was left-handed; he also had to keep his sword arm free, so his armies had to march on the right, and all of French-conquered continental Europe had to follow suit. From then onwards any part of the world colonized by the Brits drove on the left, and the parts of the world colonized by the Europeans drove on the right. Except for Japan. The mostly right-handed Samurai warriors quickly worked out that it paid to ride or walk on the left to keep the sword arm free. In the USA, the first law requiring drivers to keep right was passed in Pennsylvania in 1792, and similar laws were passed in New York in 1804 and New Jersey in 1813.

Driving on the left is absolutely right for about a quarter of the world, including Australia.

Who's Left?

Anguilla, Antigua & Barbuda, Australia, Bahamas, Bangladesh, Barbados, Bermuda, Bhutan, Botswana, British Virgin Islands, Brunei, Cayman Islands, Channel Islands, Cyprus, Dominica, Falkland Islands, Fiji, Grenada, Guyana. Hong Kong, India, Indonesia, Isle of Man, Jamaica, Japan, Kenya, Lesotho, Macau, Malawi, Malaysia, Malta, Mauritius, Montserrat, Mozambique, Namibia, Nepal, New Zealand, Pakistan, Papua New Guinea, Republic of Ireland, Seychelles, Singapore, Solomon Islands, South Africa, Sri Lanka, St Kitts & Nevis, St Helena, St Lucia, Surinam, Swaziland, St Vincent & the Grenadines, Tanzania, Thailand, Tonga, Trinidad and Tobago, Turks and Caicos Islands, Uganda, United Kingdom, US Virgin Islands, Zambia and Zimbabwe.

'Any Color, So Long As It's Black'

There are at least two versions of the quote attributed to Henry Ford about the colour of the 'Tin Lizzie' Model T – they are: 'People can have the Model T in any color – so long as it's black.' Or 'Any customer can have a car painted any color that he wants so long as it is black.' Over time this has been corrupted to become the most quoted line in automotive history – 'Any color, so long as it's black.' However, we can find no evidence the venerable Henry ever actually said it. What he did though was invent a production line to build his 'car for the masses' and thus lay the foundations for what many regard as the second

A Model T rolls out of the factory. The photo is monochrome, but it doesn't matter because so was the car.

Motor Mania

Industrial Revolution. The Ford Motor Company built an astonishing 15 million Model T-based cars between 1908 and 1927 – with very few changes to the original design. The affectionate 'Tin Lizzie' name arose from the lightweight sheet steel used in the car's construction. By that token, Volvos should probably be called 'Iron Ingas'.

Diesel Breakdown

In 1892, German engineer Rudolf Diesel was granted a patent for a new internal combustion engine, in which the fuel–air mixture would be compressed so much that ignition could take place without the aid of a spark. The invention of the diesel engine made Diesel a multi-millionaire by the time he was 40 in 1898. He built a magnificent mansion, bought a Mercedes racing car and generally lived the high life. But a series of bad investments, a law suit and the expiration of his patent saw all those millions and more disappear. On 29 September 1913 he boarded the steamer SS *Dresden* bound for England. Despite his troubles he was said to be in good spirits. When he didn't appear for breakfast, the ship was searched. Diesel's cabin was empty, the bed had not been slept in and his luggage had not been opened. His coat and hat were found neatly arranged. The inventor's diary had a small cross under 29 September and that was all. On 10 October, a Belgian steamer *Coertsen* spotted a body in the water. It was Diesel.

Red or Dead

The UK lays claim to the world's first traffic lights. They were invented by J. P. Knight, a railway-signal engineer, and installed in 1868 to control the horse-drawn traffic chaos near the Houses of Parliament. The signal consisted of red and green semaphore arms, just like the railway signals of the time. Gas-lit and hand operated by a policeman, they were taken down a year later after an explosion seriously injured the operator.

Crystal Balls-up

On 17 August 1896, 44-year-old mother-of-two Bridget Driscoll became the first person in the world to be killed by a moving car. She was killed on a terrace in the grounds of London's Crystal Palace by a car owned the Anglo-French Motor Carriage (Roger-Benz) Company that was being used to give demonstration rides to the public. The driver, Arthur Edsell, an employee of the company, had been driving for only three weeks and had tampered with the car's drive belts 'causing it to go at twice the intended speed'. At the time of the accident Edsell was said to have been distracted by the young lady passenger beside him. No action was taken by the police. However, at the inquest the coroner said, 'I trust that this sort of nonsense must never happen again.'

A Brief History of Firsts

Airbag Inventor Allen Breed patented his crash-sensing 'sensor and safety system' in 1968. It was the world's first electromechanical automobile airbag system. The 1973 Oldsmobile Toronado was the first car with an airbag intended for sale to the public. And with front-wheel drive, a huge Detroit V8 engine and terrible handling, it needed it.

Air Conditioning The Packard Motor Car Company marketed a car with air conditioning as an optional extra in 1939 for $274.00. The compressor was belt-driven off the engine, but the system had no thermostat to control the temperature. The cold air was discharged from the rear of the cabin. The car's occupants were said by sceptics to have the choice of being frozen or boiled. No change there, then.

Asphalt Although asphalt blocks were used in 1824 to pave the Champs-Elysées in Paris, the first modern road asphalt was the work of a Belgian immigrant to the USA, Edward de Smedt. By 1872 he had engineered 'a well-graded' maximum-density asphalt. This new road asphalt was first used in the same year in Battery Park and Fifth Avenue in New York City. Very posh.

Battery The first practical lead-acid battery that could be recharged was developed by French physicist Gaston Planté in 1859. It's still the car battery of choice almost a century and a half later. And it still goes flat. In the UK the Automobile Association responds to an average of 1650 flat-battery call-outs every day.

Cruise Control We may think of it as one of the 'toys' fitted to today's high-spec motors, but cruise control was patented in 1945 by blind American inventor Ralph Teetor, who was said to have thought up the idea after a jerky car ride. Chrysler was first with cruise control in 1958 when it was offered with the Imperial, New Yorker and Windsor models.

8-track Tape In-car entertainment of the audio kind took a quantum leap in September 1965 when Ford of America offered 8-track tape players as an option on every one of the company's 1966 models. Invented by William Lear of Lear Jet fame, the 8-track player was developed by a consortium of Ampex magnetic tapes, Lear Jet aircraft and RCA Records. The tapes sounded great – until the machine inevitably chewed them up and spat them out.

Electric Power Windows Introduced as a luxury feature on top-of-the-range Daimlers in 1948, power windows did not appear on more popular cars until the 1960s. Ralph Nader, the high-profile public-interest watchdog, referred to power windows as 'guillotines' after Detroit Mayor Jerome Cavanaugh's two-year-old son Christopher was caught in the tailgate power window of the family's new station-wagon and nearly strangled.

Fuel Injection Mechanical fuel-injection systems were in use for diesel engines in the 1920s. In World War II the concept was adapted for petrol-powered aircraft. US company Bendix developed an electronic fuel-injection system for cars in the early 1950s, but it proved to be expensive and impractical, and the patents were sold to German firm Bosch. The brilliant, gull-wing Mercedes-Benz supercar of 1955, the 300SL, was the first petrol fuel-injected production car, using a mechanical system made by Bosch.

Internal Combustion Engine – Four Stroke Although Nikolaus August Otto patented the four-stroke 'Otto Cycle' in 1876, the four-stroke principle of induction, compression, ignition, exhaust was actually figured out by Alphonse Beau de Rochas in 1862. Alphonse had neglected – or had forgotten – to apply for a patent. Messrs Daimler and Benz were subsequently successful in breaking the Otto patent by claiming a legal something called 'prior art' from Alphonse. Sneaky.

Internal Combustion Engine – Two Stroke Nasty, smelly and annoyingly noisy, especially in pizza delivery mopeds late at night, the cheap-to-make and very simple two-stroke was coincidentally also invented in 1876 by Sir Douglas Clerk. Sometimes called the 'Clerk Cycle' engine, it was patented in 1881. It got its 'two-stroke' name because it provides a power-stroke every second stroke.

Mileometer (Odometer) In 1847, Mormon William Clayton, with help from Orson Pratt, invented the mechanical odometer, in which individual gears control each digit. They called it the 'Roadometer' and used it to count the revolutions of the wheels of pioneer wagons. The Roadometer had multiple gears, including one that turned every quarter-mile and another that turned every ten miles – just like those in use today.

Number Plates (License Plates) Car number plates were introduced in France by the French police in 1893. The USA was next in 1901 when the state of New York became the first to require licence plates by law. The UK number-plate system was introduced in 1903, starting with 'A1'. The first owner of A1, Earl Russell, had queued all night outside the London County Council offices in order to secure the plate.

Parking Meter You might think that the authorities use parking meters and the latest 'pay and display' machines as a licence to print money, but the original idea was introduced in response to the problems of city parking congestion by American inventor Carlton Cole Magee. His 'Park-O-Meter' was patented in 1935, and he set up the Magee-Hale Park-O-Meter company to manufacture the machines. They did cause a bit of aggro in the early days – vigilantes from Alabama and Texas attempted to destroy the machines *en masse*.

Seat Belts New Yorker Edward J. Claghorn was granted a patent for an automobile safety belt in 1885. His 'Safety Belt for Tourists' is described in the US patent as 'designed to be applied to the person, and provided with hooks and other attachments for securing the person to a fixed object'. The complex leather straps and metal-buckled device looked like something out of a sado-masochist's dream. Once buckled up, the victim would not have been able to move a muscle. The modern three-point lap-and-diagonal seat belt was devised by Swedish inventor Nils Bohlin and was first used by Volvo in 1959. Clunk-click.

Speedometer The curved-dash American Oldsmobile of 1901 was the first car to be fitted with a speedometer. By 1908 speedometers were available on many cars as an expensive option. Overland offered the first car with a speedometer as standard, followed by Cadillac. The first British speedometer was developed by Samuel Smith, who founded Smiths Instruments Limited in 1904. Conspiracy theorists reckon that speedometers have always been calibrated to be around 10 per cent fast in an attempt to get drivers to obey speed limits.

Turbocharger In 1905 the Swiss engineer Dr Alfred J. Büchi was granted the first patent for a practical turbocharger – a supercharger driven by an engine's exhaust gases. In 1915, as chief engineer of Sulzer Brothers research department, Dr Büchi supervised the building of the first prototype of a turbocharged diesel engine – but it didn't work well enough to maintain a usable boost pressure. Turbocharged diesel engines appeared on trucks and buses in 1957 and the first turbocharged petrol engines in production cars appeared in the 1962 Oldsmobile Jetfire Turbo Rocket and the Chevrolet Corvair flat-six – and thus the motoring term 'turbo-lag' was coined. They proved to be somewhat unreliable and the car world had to wait for Saab to introduce the first reliable turbocharger in the 1977 Saab 99 Turbo.

The Wheel We'd get nowhere fast without our wheels. But who came up with the idea in the first place? Nobody knows. It could well have been the people of Mesopotamia over 6000 years ago because a wheel was found in an archeological dig in Iraq and is believed to be over 5500 years old.

Windscreen (Windshield) Wipers Ladies can cheer – we have a female inventor at last. American Mary Anderson was granted her first patent for a window-cleaning device in 1903. The invention was able to clear rain, sleet or snow from a windscreen by moving a handle inside a car. It consisted of a rubber blade on a swinging arm operated by a lever within the vehicle. She was said to have had the idea during a trip to New York when she noticed that streetcar drivers had to open the windows of their vehicles when it rained in order to see where they were going. By 1916 windscreen wipers were standard equipment on all American cars.

The Italian Job

The Lingotto factory in the centre of Turin was both the birthplace and headquarters of Fiat. Built in the 1920s, the 500-metre-long, five-storey building was the first example of modular construction in

Fiat's Lingotto factory featured a test track on the roof so the cars could break down close to home.

reinforced concrete. It was also the first and only car factory with a test track on the roof – as seen briefly in the getaway sequence in the original *The Italian Job* movie. When Fiat stopped production in the Lingotto in 1983 the building's importance to Turin was such that it was given a new lease of life as a multi-purpose business and cultural centre with an auditorium, an exhibition centre, a branch of the university, a shopping centre, the luxury Meridian Lingotto hotel and a 2600-seat cinema. Fiat has kept its headquarters in the building and the test track is still in use – for joggers.

Drive In, Make Out

In 1950s America you took your date to a drive-in movie. Fifties cars had bench seats that made necking and petting at the drive-in a feature of the period. Some pundits even correlate the decline of the drive-in to the introduction of bucket seats. The biggest ever drive-in was the All-Weather Drive-In in Copiague, New York. It had parking space for 2500 cars, an indoor 1200-seat viewing area, a children's playground, a restaurant – and a shuttle train to get movie-goers to and from the covered complex. The two smallest drive-ins were the Harmony Drive-In of Harmony, Pennsylvania, and the Highway Drive-In of Bamberg, South Carolina. Both drive-ins could hold no more than 50 cars.

Push Me-Pull Me

The tandem-seat three-wheel Messerschmitt KR200 Kabinenroller (cabin scooter) was built by the famous German aeroplane company from 1955 to 1964. Looking like a streamlined fighter-plane cockpit on wheels and nicknamed 'Cinderella's Coffin' because of the lack of protection afforded to the driver and passenger, the KR200 boasted a feature unseen on any volume production car before or since. To go into reverse, the engine was stopped, and the ignition key turned and held to the left. This re-started the two-stroke single-cylinder Sachs engine in reverse rotation – it also meant that all the gears were available in reverse. In theory it could go backwards at its maximum speed of around 60mph. (Berg Sr owned a KR200 in the early 1960s but was never brave enough – or idiotic enough – to try it.)

An Early Warning?

In 1930s Germany, Adolf Hitler was at the height of constructing his autobahns. But one particular stretch of new road caused chaos in his new world order. At kilometre marker 239 more than 100 cars crashed in the first year, with nine cars crashing on a single day in September 1930. The road was completely straight and flat, and no explanation could be given for the accidents. Only when the marker was removed and the area sprinkled with holy water did the crashes stop.

Why are We Stopping?

The world's first traffic jam happened in Washington, DC, on 11 November 1921 – Armistice Day. It lasted three hours and involved 3000 vehicles. The jam began as a procession of world leaders led by President Warren G. Harding drove from the US Capitol to Arlington National Cemetery to bury the Unknown Soldier. As the procession drove across the Potomac river towards the cemetery the traffic ground to a halt. The cemetery had no car-parking facilities and the fields surrounding it were filled with cars. There was nowhere for the remaining traffic to go. The world's first traffic jam was a revelation. The cars that were rolling off Henry Ford's production lines promised freedom and mobility. The idea that they could be trapped for hours in stationary queues stunned Washington. In the enquiry that followed, the police blamed the army, which was in charge of the Armistice Day programme, and the army blamed the police. Police Superintendent Gessford took the blame from the press and public after it emerged that he had assigned just three police officers to control traffic. Gessford resigned within weeks. His obituary years later said that the 'calamity caused an immediate breakdown in his health'.

Not exactly The Ultimate Driving Machine, the BMW Isetta 'Bubble' car had no reverse, and left drivers stranded if they parked too close to a wall.

The Great Escape

The BMW Isetta 'Bubble' car, built from 1956 to 1962, shared its front-opening-door design with Heinkel's three-wheel Cabin Cruiser. However, to save costs, the Isetta had no reverse gear. Drivers taking advantage of small parking spaces often parked the car front-end-on to the kerb – and then couldn't open the door. Fortunately the Isetta had a folding canvas sunroof, thus affording the trapped driver a viable, if ungainly and sometimes embarrassing, exit.

Slow Coaches

Just 2mph in towns and 4mph everywhere else – and a pedestrian had to walk in front carrying a red flag. Yep, the first speed limit became law in 1865 in the UK and lasted until 1896, when it was increased to 14mph. It was increased again in 1903 to 20mph. And in 1930 all speed limits for cars and motorcycles were abolished. The freedom lasted just four years when a 30mph limit was imposed on roads in built-up areas. National speed limits were unknown in the USA, where individual states set their own limits. In 1909 the state of Washington imposed a 12mph limit in built-up areas and 24mph out of town. The state speed limit is currently 70mph, and it's illegal to 'embrace another while driving'. Another what?

In a Hurry, Sir?

On 20 May 1899 electric-taxicab driver Jacob German became the first American driver to be arrested for speeding when he was chased and stopped by bicycle patrolman Schueller for driving at the 'break-neck' speed of 12mph on Lexington Avenue in Manhattan, New York. Did the cop's bike have a speedometer? The first person to be convicted of speeding in the UK was John Henry Knight. In 1895 he was convicted for exceeding the 4mph speed limit in his self-built 12mph three-wheel two-seater. Shame, because just one year later the limit was increased to 14mph. Again, how did they know? Maybe the policeman had to break into a trot to catch him. His car also happened to be the first British petrol-driven road vehicle.

Ton Up

Frenchman Louis Rigolly was the first man to drive at over 100mph. He set a record of 103.561mph on a beach at Ostend in Belgium on 21 July 1904, driving a 13.5-litre Gobron-Brillé racing car. The record lasted just three months. A Darracq car driven by another Frenchman, Paul Baras, set a new record of 104.530mph on 13 November, also at Ostend. The first 100mph production car was the 125-hp, 3.5-litre, six-cylinder, 1938 Jaguar SS100. It cost £445. We'll have one each, please.

Jam Sandwich

A German truck driver made history in August 2004 when he caused what is believed to be the world's first traffic jam caused by jam. He was trying to swat a wasp that had got into his cab and lost control of his jam-packed truck and smashed into the barrier on the A1 autobahn near the town of Greven. The truck's 15-ton load spilled on to the road covering it with jam – which attracted swarm after swarm of wasps. The police had to close the motorway for two hours while the mess was cleaned up – causing a long traffic, er, jam.

THREE

Motorworld

Foreigners are funny. They're not like us and they certainly don't drive like us, as this chapter makes perfectly plain. We've scoured the globe (well, the internet anyway) and unearthed the weirdest, most wonderful – and occasionally worrying – tales, and the craziest cars, from the world of motoring to give you an insight into what it's like on the road abroad. After this you'll be glad you stayed at home.

North America

THE UNITED STATES

Bum Steer – The Naked Classic-Car Show

The annual classic-car show at the Valley View Recreation Club just outside the village of Cambridge, Wisconsin, would never have made it on to the *Top Gear* radar if it weren't for one minor detail: all the exhibitors are butt naked. Held every August, and celebrating its seventeenth year in 2006, the Nude Car Show is a mix of hot metal and burnt buttocks. *Top Gear*'s own Andy Wilman visited in 1998 with a camera crew and a photographer, and his blushes were broadcast to the millions of viewers of the world's most popular TV car programme. With oversized American women proudly displaying gleaming headlamps and men polishing knobs for the judges, it makes uncomfortable watching. But not nearly as uncomfortable as Wilman's sudden discovery that leather seats, the Wisconsin sun and his proud British buttocks do not mix.

Wisconsin's Nude Car Show – an uncomfortable mix of hot cars and burnt buttocks.

Clowning Around

One of the silliest ideas boffins have ever dreamed up has to be the one that was, according to *New Scientist* magazine, part of a serious road-safety project at the T. J. Watson research labs in New York. Researchers wanted to arouse drowsy drivers by squirting water in their faces from a computer installed in the car's dashboard. And if that weren't enough the computer would also tell jokes. We kid you not. The prototype IBM Artificial Passenger was a computer with video eyes, microphone ears, a sniff-sensor nose and a loud voice. It measured a driver's eye-blink rate and head position, and sniffed for alcohol or drugs. If the driver's head drooped or blink-rate slowed the computer would decide to check the state of tiredness by telling a joke or asking a question. Failure to respond in an adequate fashion would prompt a liberal dousing of water, presumably followed by custard pie.

Mine's Bigger than Yours

US car customizers have been 'stretching' luxury sedans since the 1930s. In case you didn't know, stretching involves cutting a vehicle in half and inserting an additional centre section, usually between 3 and 5 metres long. The most popular stretch limo, now seen in almost every capital city in the world, is based on the Lincoln Town car, stretched to take from six to 14 passengers. But the stretchers seem unable to stop themselves stretching the most unlikely cars. Robert Strausser (known as 'Limo Bob'), based in Palos Hills, Chicago, built the record-breaking articulated 73-metre-long Patriot and specializes in stretching and fitting out the most outrageous vehicles: a Ford Excursion Diplomat for rap star Eminem and a stretch Hummer with a casino in the back for a British customer. He has even fitted cars with putting greens and swimming pools.

Haunted Highways

America is home to more ghostly goings-on than anywhere else in the world. It's hard to name its eeriest avenue, but Highway 49 in California does link several of the country's most haunted houses. Vineyard House, near Coloma, is home to the ghost of Robert Chambers who starved himself to death in 1879. It's now a hotel, if you fancy a visit with a visitation. Further up the road at Mokelume Hill is the Hotel Leger. Former owner George Leger still walks the halls, even though he's long dead. The Sutter Inn, just a few miles further north, houses a whole family of spectres and their guests. Just the road trip for Scooby-Doo and the gang.

Car Sailsman

Is it a boat? Is it an RV? Nope, it's both. It's the world's first and only motor-home that's almost as mobile on water as it is on the highway. It's billed by its maker as the 'world's first luxury amphibious motor coach yacht'. It's claimed to be capable of 7kn (8mph) in seas with swells as high as 3 feet. In the final production version the power for road use is a 500hp diesel. In the water, marine diesels up to 300hp can be specified to drive the twin propellers. For sea-going stability, twin hydraulically operated sponsons take the width up from 8 foot 6 inches to 17 feet.

Made by CAMI LLC in South Carolina, the Terra Wind has a Jacuzzi, 60-inch bathtub, marble floors, leather furniture, mirrored ceilings, granite counter tops and all residential appliances, including a 22-cubic-foot side-by-side refrigerator with ice and water in the door, a four-burner glass hob, combination microwave/convection oven, a dishwasher, trash compactor and a washer/dryer combination. Just like luxury motor yachts, the Terra Wind is built to order and costs from $850,000 to a piffling $1,200,000. In case you were wondering, CAMI stands for Cool Amphibious Manufacturers International (and LLC means Limited Liability Company, just so you're fully in the know).

It's a Bling Thing

Stateside hip-hop stars and overpaid big-name athletes think little of prettying up their Humvees and jacked-up Cadillac Escalades with a $15,000 set of Asanti alloys. Sister company Lexani Wheels goes even further by offering luxury alloys inset with 150-carat zirconia gemstones in green, clear red and yellow. Asanti jacked up the ante in 2004 with a set of hand-made alloys for the Rolls-Royce Phantom, at the time the world's most expensive alloys at a whopping $250,000. Each wheel has 21 princess-cut zirconia stones hand-set by a jeweller. Top that? Well, yes, because in 2005 Asanti revealed a set of 1100-carat-diamond-encrusted alloys hand-set by jewellers IceLink for the Bentley GT, for the bargain-basement price of $1 million. Customers get the Bentley free of charge.

Baby Beemers

Brooke Wheeler, editor of San Francisco BabyCentre.com, took it upon himself to compile a list of babies born in 2005 whose petrol-head parents saddled them with the names of cars. From the data sent in by 320,000 BabyCenter members he came up with:

Boys: *Lincoln, Royce, Ford, Bentley, Chevy, Kia, Benz, Scion, Beemer, Chrysler*

Girls: *Mercedes, Lexus, Lotus, Chevy, Kia, Royce, Porsche, Infiniti, Chrysla*

Car Henge

Deep in the Texas panhandle, in a wheat field west of Amarillo, the motoring equivalent of Stonehenge stands in silent tribute to America's once finest automobile. It's a line of ten half-buried Cadillacs, ranging, in chronological order, from a 1949 Club Coupé to a 1963 Sedan

Cadillac Ranch. Built by ancient druids or tripped-out hippies – what do you think?

de Ville, noses down, rear wheels upended, tail fins pointing skywards towards Cadillac heaven. In 1974 a San Francisco collective of artists calling themselves Ant Farm decided to create a unique open-air sculptural tribute to the Cadillac. Three decades on, Cadillac Ranch is now a rusting, vandalized shadow of its former gleaming glory. Graffiti covers the paintwork, all the windows have been smashed, and souvenir hunters have removed the chrome trim, the radios, the speakers and even some of the doors.

Save the Earth with a Hummer

When the Rotary Club of Chatham in Miramichi, Canada, decided to try and raise $100,000 for the French Fort Cove Eco-Center, they quite conventionally came up with a raffle. But the prize was the Greens' top hate machine the H2 Hummer. Local critics said, 'Anyone with environmental awareness wouldn't be caught dead behind the wheel of a Hummer.' Nevertheless, Leon Bremner, who helped organize the raffle, said the Hummer drew a lot of attention, and that's just what was needed to sell tickets. He also said, 'Hummers aren't any harder on gas than many other big trucks and SUVs.'

Red Bull's Revenge

In July 2005, on US Highway 395 in Douglas County, Nevada, Red, an aptly named bull, charged, gouged and head-butted a line of road-maintenance workers' parked cars. The local sheriff's office said that two of the workers managed to get a towrope around Red's neck and tie him to their truck. Red then promptly attacked the truck. The damage was estimated at $6400, but Nevada law protects cattle owners from liability in a collision between a vehicle and cattle on roads in open-range areas, so Red got away scot-free.

Sacred Saabs and Holy Hondas

Once a year in Los Feliz, Los Angeles, California, members of the Minxes all-female car club take their cars to an all-day and well-into-the-night event called The Blessing of the Cars. Organized by classic-car lovers Stephanie and Gabriel Baltierra, the event has grown from just a few hundred friends and their cars to more than 10,000. The event begins in the morning with a mass blessing by a Catholic priest, before each car receives an individual blessing. Holy water is available for radiators on request.

Driving Miss Crazy

Linda Sajero of Denver, Colorado, is probably America's worst driver. She has been involved in 117 accidents. She has run over 18 dogs, 11 cats and nine deer and driven right through her house, entering at the front door and leaving through a back wall. Her most successful roadkill manoeuvre was achieved when she reversed out of her drive at 45mph, hitting three stray dogs at once. She managed to hit the only tree on a 2-mile stretch of straight road, killed a cat when swerving to avoid a rattlesnake and survived a 300-foot drop over a cliff in the Rockies – landing on top of a deer. Linda says that she doesn't want to give up the independence that driving gives her, 'but I keep thinking if I just keep practising, someday I'll be able to drive like a normal person.'

Dubya's de Ville

The most powerful man in the world, the US President, rides around in a heavily armoured stretched Cadillac de Ville. The exact specification is top secret, but security experts believe that the body is bullet-proofed with Kevlar, the underside is bomb-proof and the side windows are made of thick polycarbonate. Special run-flat tyres will keep the car drivable even if all four are shot out. In the event of chemical or biological attack, 'Cadillac One', as it has been dubbed, can seal its cabin and rely on its own air supply. And, if the headlamps should be shot out during a night attack the driver can rely on night-vision technology.

Mower Man

College soccer coach Brad Hauter set a Guinness world record in 1999 for driving an 18-hp lawn mower from Los Angeles, California, to New York City in 600 hours – a distance of 3976 miles. The maximum speed of his 'Yard-Man' motor mower is around 25mph. He probably got the idea from Iowan Alvin Straight, who in 1994, at the age of 73, drove his 5mph 'John Deere' lawn mower 240 miles from Laurens, Iowa, to Mount Zion, Wisconsin, to visit his ailing 80-year-old brother. The journey took six weeks and became the subject of David Lynch's movie *The Straight Story*.

South America

BOLIVIA

Drive Carefully

Bolivia holds the dubious honour of being home to The World's Most Dangerous Road. Known as El Camino del Muerte, Death Road, it drops 3000 metres in less than 70 km, winding its way down the mountain from La Paz, through waterfalls, around landslides, past thick rainforest and down to the Coca plantations that surround Coroico – without a crash barrier in sight. In many places the gravel track is only one car wide and the vertigo-inducing drops spell the end for anyone unfortunate enough to get it wrong. It's the only road in South America where traffic drives on the left so that vehicles travelling uphill hug the mountainside. (In left-hand-drive vehicles the driver can look out

A typical roadside picnic on El Camino del Muerte (Death Road) in Bolivia.

of the window and see the edge.) Native Aymara Indian sorcerers do a roaring trade, charging around $40 to bless your journey. Around half a dozen people actually live out on the road serving as human traffic lights on the most treacherous sections, relying on handouts from grateful drivers. Nevertheless, there are scores of accidents every year. And having driven the road ourselves we can understand why.

BRAZIL

One Lump or Two?

Sugar is the fuel of the future in Brazil. And, curiously, of the past as well. During the 1980s, ethanol made from sugar cane was introduced and thanks to government subsidies proved hugely popular. But a drop in oil prices meant that throughout the 1990s Brazil gradually moved back to petrol power. In 2003 that all changed again. With a more favourable tax and cheaper fuel for ethanol-run cars, the Brazilians have embraced sugar-power once more. In 2005, over 50 per cent of new cars sold were designed to run on the fuel. It's cheap and carbon neutral as planting new crops negates the burning of the fuel. Sweet.

Stating the Obvious

Spawned from the sweet success of cheap ethanol power comes the Obvio! 828 – Brazil's answer to the Smart Car. The strangely punctuated city vehicle seats three, has a mid-mounted 1.6-litre engine driving the rear wheels and is small enough to be parked frontways, Smart-style. The funky plastic body hides a steel shell that employs an aeronautical specification 'Niess Elliptical' survival cell. It can run on 100 per cent ethanol and deliver up to 250hp, although standard output is 115hp. It goes on sale in 2007 for $14,000, and we want one.

Red-light Robbery

Drivers in Rio de Janeiro were told in 1999 that they could run red lights at night in a bid to cut down on the city's car-jacking epidemic. Police said that as long as drivers slowed for the lights they would not be fined between 10 p.m. and 5 a.m. This flexible approach was introduced after a clampdown on driving standards had reduced the road death toll, but increased the number of drivers being targeted by criminals.

CHILE

Bumper Kiss

Chilean car lovers got to prove their passion in December 2004. In a competition run by the radio station Rock and Pop Santiago, 28 people took part in a car-kissing challenge. The winner, 22-year-old José Aliaga, received the keys to the new car after his final rival fainted. He'd been snogging the motor for an astonishing 54 hours 22 minutes. Aliaga was only allowed one 7-minute break every 3 hours during the marathon.

COLOMBIA

Pablo Escobar: Car Addict

Notorious drugs baron Pablo Escobar was a major car junkie. He started his criminal career boosting cars and by the time he'd reached the dizzy heights of number-one most wanted criminal, he'd built up a $4-million car collection that included Al Capone's car. Escobar also reportedly gave away numerous cars to ladies who took part in naked running races at his ranch Hacienda Napoles.

MEXICO

Hi-tech Smog Check

Mexico City is one of the world's most polluted cities. Sitting in a natural basin more than 7400 feet above sea level, a thick layer of smog hangs over it for most of the year, choking its 20 million residents. Mexico City's ozone levels typically exceed World Health Organization standards on 300 days each year. Numerous efforts to reduce pollution from cars have been tried – including banning up to 40 per cent of vehicles from the roads. Some of the more unusual attempts to clean the city include trialling compressed-air-powered taxis and using radio waves to blast away ozone.

PARAGUAY

The President's Bent BMW

Paraguay's president Luis González Macchi was caught driving a stolen BMW 7-Series in 2001. Police estimate that more than half the cars in Paraguay are stolen in other countries and sneaked over the border. Macchi claimed he didn't know his car was stolen but the scandal forced the resignation of three government ministers. The president held his position until 2003, after his interior minister pointed out that journalists, priests and even police drove stolen cars as well. Doh!

Europe

FRANCE

A Tree Hit My Car

Some of the best insurance-claim-form excuses we've happened upon are those compiled by the Insurance Information and Statistics Centre (CDIA) in Paris. Here are ten of our favourites:

1. I am a little hard of hearing so you can understand why I didn't see the cyclist.

2. I admit I went through the intersection without looking to see if anyone was crossing, but I had gone through the same intersection less than an hour before and no-one was there.

3. In place of the intersection they built a roundabout with priority for those coming from the left. Now I didn't expect that change and I lost control of my car.

4. While going forward I smashed the rear light of the car in front of me. So I backed up, and in doing so smashed the bumper of the car behind me. That's when I stepped out of the car, but in doing so I knocked down a bicyclist with my door. That's all I have to declare for today.

5. I rammed into a parked car and made sure not to tell the owner that I was responsible. I hope you are satisfied with me and will award me additional bonus points on my insurance.

6. I am stunned that you refuse to pay for this accident on grounds that I wasn't wearing my glasses. I swear the accident wasn't my fault. I simply didn't see the bicyclist when I ran him over.

7. I drove into the wrong house and collided with a tree I don't have.

8. The accident happened because I had one eye on the truck in front, one eye on the pedestrian, and the other on the car behind.

9. I consider neither vehicle to blame, but if either was to blame it was the other one.

10. An invisible car came out of nowhere, struck my car and vanished.

GERMANY

Punk My Ride

It had to come. It's the car's equivalent of Punk's obsession with body piercing. The Claudia Geisler paint-shop in Delmenhorst, between Oldenburg and Bremen, Germany, will, for around 166 euros, pierce your motor and insert the very latest in automotive jewellery – a see-through sealed enclosure that displays your own ornamental icon. Suggestions include a Barbie Doll, an Action Man, photographs, or even a scale model of the car itself. According to our source (Jalopnik), 'carpunkers' have the op done on their car's bonnet, or boot, but the word is that some jokey Germans are showing up at Berlin's weird-gigs platz, Maria am Ostbahnhof, with bits of communist-era Trabants stuck through their windscreens.

Restoration Comedy

The Trabant, the made-out-of-papier-mâché, underpowered, two-stroke polluter-car made in communist East Germany, is having a new lease of life – as a 'car experience'. German company 'Trabi-Safari' runs Trabi trips for tourists in Berlin and Dresden. You can have a 'Trabi Experience' in any one of 15 restored cars, ranging from what is probably the world's only stretched, six-wheel open-top Trabant to saloons, estates and a Trabi 'Limo'. The mind boggles.

GREECE

Traffic Calming

Greek police gave away free folk-music CDs in an attempt to soothe drivers in the annual Orthodox Easter exodus from Athens in 2005. The CDs came with a copy of the highway code, maps and a Happy Easter message from the public-order minister. Wonder how many accidents were caused by people driving while messing around with their CD players?

Gregorios Sachinidis's 1976 Mercedes taxi has done 2.8 million miles. And he never once went south of the river.

Taxi to the Moon

Greek taxi driver Gregorios Sachinidis finally had enough of his 1976 Mercedes 240D in 2004, so he sent it back to its makers. Sachinidis from Thessaloniki had driven 2.8 million miles. That's as far as the moon and back or 82 times around the world – the furthest distance by a single car on record. His car is now in Mercedes's museum in Stuttgart, Germany.

HOLLAND

Polyurethane Dreams

Here's something for all you would-be car designers – maybe. Dutch designer Marijn van der Poll has come up with what he calls 'The Modular Car'. He provides a rolling chassis, complete with engine, gearbox and control essentials, and surrounds it with a cube of polyurethane foam. You design your dream car by carving the foam block into the desired shape with a saw – finishing it off with sandpaper. You then get the thing laminated in glassfibre and polyester resin. The result we've seen looks like a block of foam, laminated in glassfibre and polyester resin, on wheels and with a colourful paint job.

ITALY

Roman Road Rage

A double-parker in Rome who parked 'in such a way that another motorist could not move his car' was deemed worthy of an act of 'private violence' by Italy's Supreme Court in 2004. The Rome resident, identified only as Luigi C., was found guilty of trapping motorist Michele C. in February 2004. The penalty was 15 days in jail and a fine of 500 euros. The jail sentence was suspended, but Luigi C. had to pay the fine, plus court costs.

POLAND

The DIY SLR

Polish church historian Robert Furtak watched the launch of the Mercedes-Benz SLR at the 1999 Detroit Motor Show on TV and immediately decided to make one himself. He got hold of a copy of the Merc press kit, magazine photographs and, most importantly, a one-eighteenth-scale Maestro model of the car. What happened next is an almost unbelievable tale of craft, skill and determination. Every part of the scale model was measured with callipers and the measurements multiplied by 18. Then, with the help of master car-body builder Feliks Ciask, each piece was made full size and the body assembled on to a crashed donor 21-year-old Mercedes-Benz 500 SEC chassis. Four years of remarkable DIY later, the SLR was finished – and road legal. The DIY SLR is probably worth more than the real thing at an estimated 75,000 euros, and Mr Furtak says that it is his old-age pension.

ROMANIA

Blow Out

A 19-year-old Romanian man crashed while his girlfriend gave him oral sex in the centre of Craiova, Romania, in 2005. Robert Filip 'forgot' to make a turn and crashed into a parked car. Undeterred by the accident, the couple carried on romping until the police arrived. Filip was banned from driving for 90 days and had to pay for damage to the parked car but was not prosecuted. If you ask us, he was very lucky. Ever read John Irving's *The World According to Garp*?

RUSSIA

It's the Bisnis

Russian politicos, 'bisnismen', bankers, oil billionaires, Russki mafia godfathers and anybody else in Russia needing the protection of an armoured vehicle need look no further than the home-grown Combat T-98 luxury 4×4 from St Petersburg-based Kombat Armoring. This is one fearsome beast – we haven't seen anything like it since the 1970s Lamborghini LM. It's the fastest all-road armoured vehicle in the world with a 340bhp V8 engine taking it to a maximum speed of 111mph. And it's got all the toys: sat-nav, DVD, flat-screen TV, climate control, leather-and-wood interior. Should be reliable too, all the running gear and electronics are supplied by General Motors. The makers say that the 3750-kg vehicle will protect occupants against 12.7mm bullets, shotgun blasts, mines and attempts at ramming.

Volga – No Longer Vulga

Russia's mundane, much joked-about Volga has been transformed. The humble Soviet-era workhorse now has the looks of a modern-ish, low and wide, cool Yank coupé – complete with loads of 1950s-style chrome. With a 380-bhp V12 engine courtesy of BMW and running gear and interior from a Beemer 850, the Volga looks the business. It also goes as fast as it looks, with a maximum speed of 160mph plus.

Own the Road

The special VIP lanes on Russia's roads, introduced during the Soviet era so that members of the Politburo could speed unhindered in their massive Zil limos, are alive and well in the Russia of today – and you ignore them at your peril. In February 2006, Oleg Shcherbinsky was sentenced to four years in jail for failing to get out of the way of an official Mercedes carrying the regional governor of Altay, which police said had been travelling at more than 90mph. The Mercedes clipped Oleg's Toyota, went into a skid and hit a tree, killing the Governor, his chauffeur and his bodyguard. The judge said that Oleg should have given way after seeing the limo's flashing blue lights.

Spain's Tramontana – part F1 racer, part jet fighter. Totally insane.

SPAIN

Costa Packet

Using the shape of a jet fighter as inspiration and built of aeronautical aluminium and masses of carbon fibre, the Costa Brava custom-built Tramontana is probably the most bonkers supercar we've seen outside Switzerland. The hand-built Tramontana has open wheels, open tandem seats and 500bhp, does 0–60mph in four seconds and maxes at 186mph. It's also got a maximum price: $660,000 will buy one of just 12 built every year.

TURKEY

Wash-day Warning

Be careful if you're driving on wash day in Turkey. Residents of Tokat were reported to be washing their clothes and hanging them to dry over road signs. The signs covered up on the Tokat–Sivas highway included the speed limit, a no-passing sign and a curve-ahead warning.

UNITED KINGDOM

The Mighty Atom

Steer clear of the only nuclear-power station in Wales at Wylfa if your car has remote central locking or an engine immobilizer – or both. Strange forces appear to be at work. Doors won't unlock, engines won't start – or, even stranger, doors lock and unlock repeatedly. Nuclear radiation? Alien forces? Nope. It's the radio frequency used by the perimeter security monitors to transmit information to the station's control room. It's the same one used by many car remote-control key-fobs and engine immobilizers. Most cars can still be opened manually with the key. Immobilizers are another matter. Cars have to be pushed away until they're in the station's radio shadow. The station's managers say the problem will be dealt with during 2006.

The Smart that thinks it's a Jaguar. It's still the prey for big cats in Britain's safari parks, though.

Driven round the Bend

The closest you can get to 'doing the Twist' in a car in the UK is to drive a one-mile stretch of the B3081 between Cann Common in Dorset and Tollard Royal in Wiltshire. Drive at steady 30mph (assuming that you can keep the car on the road at that speed) and according to Continental Tyres you will experience the same lateral forces as you would on a roller-coaster. The company carried out a study in 2005 to find the ten bendiest roads in Britain. Most of them are minor roads in hilly areas, the exception being the A157 in Lincolnshire, a county most people think of as being flat.

Top 10 Bendy Roads in Britain
1. *B3081 – Cann Common to Tollard Royal, Dorset/Wiltshire*
2. *A686 – Penrith to Melmerby, Cumbria*
3. *A537 – Macclesfield to Buxton, Cheshire/Derbyshire*
4. *A466 – Monmouth to Staunton, Monmouthshire*
5. *A4061 – Pricetown to Treorchy, Rhondda, Wales*
6. *A157 – Louth to Mablethorpe, Lincolnshire*
7. *B2130 – Godalming to Cranleigh, Surrey*
8. *B6270 – Keld to Reeth, North Yorkshire*
9. *A39 – Bridgwater to Minehead, Somerset*
10. *B797 – Mennock to Warnlockhead, Dumfries and Galloway*

Smart Snacks and Mini Meals

It might be small and look a bit like a toy car, but you wouldn't think a group of lionesses would mistake a Mercedes-Benz Smart for lunch. Well, they did. And staff at the Merseyside Knowsley Safari Park now have to monitor all small vehicles entering the lion enclosure. Park Manager David Ross told the BBC News website that a group of lionesses chased after a Smart car after being confused by its compact appearance. Mr Ross said: 'The lions will take an interest in peculiarities on cars and we always keep a close eye on the cars coming in. With Smart cars and sometimes Mini Coopers the lions definitely raise an eyebrow. It sparks their interest because of their size.'

Don't Drive with Tracie or Jason

According to UK online insurance company Esure, drivers named Tracie or Jason are statistically the most likely to have an accident and claim on their insurance. It could well be that for some strange reason Esure attracts more Tracies and Jasons, but more than one in three of them claim for an accident, break-in, fire or theft every year. Other 'at-risk' names are Natasha, Juliet, Natalie and Helen for women, and Lee, Sam, Alastair and Lloyd for men. Esure's safest drivers are Jacqueline, Peggy and Damon.

Africa

LIBYA

From Rocket Launchers to Rocket Cars

One-time supporter of terrorism Colonel Gaddafi has been trying to re-invent himself in recent years. And in 1999 he thought he'd have a go at car design. To celebrate 30 years of power, Gaddafi revealed the Saroukh el-Jamahiriya (Libyan Rocket). With Libya's roads and driving standards notoriously poor, the Rocket was packed full of safety features, including airbags and a collapsible bumper. 'The invention of the safest car in the world is proof that the Libyan revolution is built on the happiness of man,' said Gaddafi. Curiously, nothing has been heard of the car since its much hyped launch.

RWANDA

Don't Take the Trunk Road

War-ravaged Rwanda is hardly the safest place to be driving at the best of times, but in 2005 car travellers faced a new threat – Mutware, a bull elephant. He trashed three cars in the Akagera National Park and even prompted the US Embassy in Kigali to issue a special security warning.

SOUTH AFRICA

African Aggro

Don't cut anyone up on the road in South Africa – or else. South African drivers are the worst in the world for road rage, according to a 2005 survey. In the report, 67 per cent of South Africans said they'd been the victims of aggressive behaviour on the road, with 11 per cent saying that the aggressor had got out of the car spoiling for a fight. The survey by Synovate concluded that South Africans were 'extremely aggressive'. British drivers shouldn't be smug: the UK came second in the report with Greece taking the bullying bronze.

Jump Starts

A mysterious Mégane caused a stir in Cape Town, South Africa, in November 2004, after being witnessed jumping backwards up a hill and through a fence, despite being locked and with the handbrake on. The Renault 'ghost car' grabbed headlines throughout the country with all kinds of supernatural forces being blamed, until a mechanic discovered that a short circuit in the wiring had caused the starter motor to switch on, and with the car left in gear it bounded into action. No need to call in the Ghostbusters after all.

SWAZILAND AND MALAWI

Driving the Despots

Swaziland's King Mswati II is continuing a long tradition of African dictators by ignoring the fact that his country is one of the world's poorest and spending a fortune on cars. But having bought 15 BMWs for his wives and a Maybach 62 for himself, by 2005 he wasn't getting a very good press. So he came up with a cunning plan. He issued a royal decree banning photographers from taking pictures of him 'when he alights from his car'.

Kenya's government also came under fire for spending $12 million on new cars in four years, including 57 new Mercedes, helping to give the governing élite the Swahili nickname 'Wabenzi' (as in people who drive Benzes). In Malawi the lust for cars has filtered further down the system. In January 2005 the nation's judges went on strike when the government refused to buy them new Mercs or BMWs. Eventually, the strike was brought to an end when the powers that be agreed to cough up for some new cars – Nissan Terranos.

The Middle East

AFGHANISTAN

Satan's Wheelwomen

The Taliban of Afghanistan believed the idea of women driving was 'satanic', but in 2001, following the collaspe of the regime, women were allowed back behind the wheel after two decades of being forced into the passenger seat. The driving test isn't exactly hard – just reversing around a white line painted on the road – and many hundreds of women have taken up driving, despite the country's continuing troubles.

DUBAI

Truck's Top

Like many of Dubai's élite, Sheikh Hamdan bin Hamad Al Nahyan likes to go camping in the desert. So off he goes into the dunes in his classic 1948 Dodge Power Wagon. With its four bedrooms, four bathrooms, living room and kitchen. You see, the Sheikh's Dodge isn't exactly standard. Like many things in the Gulf, the Dodge is larger than life. Four times larger, to be precise. The 40-foot-tall truck was custom built for the Sheikh for an undisclosed sum. And if there's not enough room in the Dodge then there's always his 120-foot-long, eight-bedroom caravan (the world's largest) or the ten-bedroom Globe Car – a one-millionth scale replica of the earth, on wheels. Only in Dubai.

Showing Off

You can actually see the dealers rubbing their hands in the run-up to the annual Dubai motor show. And it's no wonder. At the 2005 show Bugatti sold no fewer than six Veyrons for a cool $1.2 million apiece in a single day. Over the course of the event a total of over $27-million worth of cars were sold.

IRAN

Hunted to Extinction

Iran's most popular car, the Paykan, was killed off in 2005 after almost 40 years. The Paykan, which means 'arrow' in Farsi, was finally axed due to its gas guzzling and smoke belching, which had become unacceptable even in one of the world's most oil-rich countries. The car, which started life in 1967 as a Hillman Hunter, struggled to better 12mpg of leaded fuel, but was a huge hit with drivers in Iran as it was so cheap. Some 40 per cent of Iranian drivers, including vast numbers of taxi operators, drive the Paykan, so the smog won't exactly disappear overnight.

The gas-guzzling Paykan was a hit with Iranian taxi drivers.

IRAQ

Dawdle and Die

Route Irish, the road between Baghdad's Green Zone and the airport, makes Bolivia's The World's Most Dangerous Road look like a village high street. It's just 12-km long but has been the location of numerous suicide bombings and shootings. Enterprising local security firms charge $3000 for a one-way taxi ride – and you'd better hope your driver doesn't hang about. The US Army's tactic is to ram with their armoured Humvees any cars witnessed being driven badly or oddly, as a preventative strike against potential suicide bombers.

JORDAN

Ample Assets

King Hussein of Jordan was one of the Middle East's biggest car nuts, as can be witnessed by the car museum in Amman opened shortly after his death. Among the, er, re-designed Range Rovers used for falconry (his other hobby), the Porsche 959, Ferrari F50 and Amphicar are a large number of Mercedes – the King's particular vehicle of choice. A 300SL Gullwing and a C111 prototype (one of only six made) are the highlights for visitors, but the King's favourite was a 1968 300SEL that he nicknamed Mabrouka (the lucky one) – it saved him from two assassination attempts, despite not being armour plated. That was back when Benzes really were built like tanks.

TURKMENISTAN

Benzes for the Masses

The people of Turkmenistan are among the poorest on the planet, despite their country's massive oil and gas deposits. But President Saparmurad Niyazov decided to make amends in 2003 by handing out free Mercedes cars to his people. Making good on a decade-old pledge that promised a house and a car for all Turkmen families, Niyazov initially gave new Mercs to ministers and top officials. The President promised new cars for them every year as long as the older cars were handed down to staff. President Niyazov, who calls himself Turkmenbashi or Father of All Turkmen, also has a Mercedes. It's a very heavily armoured car that takes him from his palace to his office down a road built especially for him.

Asia

BANGLADESH

Dhaka Daytonas

Fancy a Ferrari but can't afford supercar prices? Then pay a visit to Leepu's Garage in Dhaka. Leepu turns mundane Japanese cars into imitation Italian exotica. Leepu (real name Nizamuddin Awila) hand-makes all the body panels, using only the occasional part from Italy, such as a badge or tail light. Lamborghini and Ferrari are the most popular knock-offs, and the cost is just a fraction of the real thing. Of course, so is the performance ...

BRUNEI

Monster Garage

Until that high-tech upstart Bill Gates came along, His Majesty Sultan Haji Hassnal Bolkiah Mu'izzaddin Waddaulah the Sultan and Yang Di-Pertuan of Brunei Darussalam (the Sultan of Brunei, for short) was the richest man in the world. Thanks to his country's oil and natural gas reserves he is worth $11 billion, according to the money experts at Forbes. Despite Brunei having a road network that barely covers 1000 miles, the Sultan and his family have amassed a car collection that reputedly numbers 5000. During the 1990s the Brunei royals propped up many of the world's luxury car-makers, commissioning not just large numbers of standard models but numerous Brunei specials and one-offs as well. According to Richard Feast, author of *The Kidnap of the Flying Lady*, the Brunei royals – led by the Sultan's son Prince Jefri – purchased 70–75 Rolls-Royces and Bentleys every year between 1994 and 1997, spending up to £150 million a year and keeping Rolls-Royce afloat. Ferrari, Lamborghini, Aston Martin, Mercedes and Jaguar all benefited as well. Exact details of the Sultan's collection have never been made public, but several examples have been leaked over the years. The Sultan's specials have been supplied by:

Aston Martin Aston supplied hundreds of cars, including shooting-brakes based on the V8 Vantage- and Pininfarina-bodied AM3 and AM4 models never seen outside Brunei.

Bentley When Bentley first showed the Continental R concept car, the Brunei royals ordered a total of 23, even though it wasn't actually on sale. They also had estate, coupé and convertible versions of the Java concept and several Dominators – hybrid Range Rover–Bentley crossover vehicles at the bargain price of £1.5 million each.

Ferrari Not content with ordering scores of standard Ferraris, the Brunei royals obtained two Ferrari Mythos concept cars, had a number of unique Ferrari FX models built, based on the 512M, and commissioned convertible and estate versions of the 456 as well.

Porsche The fastest in the fleet were Dauer 962 Le Mans cars converted for road use.

Lamborghini Lamborghini's concept car was made real for Brunei. And only Brunei.

A nice hot Java – as ordered by the Sultan of Brunei from Bentley, even though they didn't officially ever make it.

Mercedes Original Mercedes 300SLs are hard to come by, so Brunei had replicas made, based on the AMG SL500. Obvious, really.

Rolls-Royce Pride of place in the fleet goes to the six stretched Rolls-Royce Phantom V limousines that cost a whopping £6 million each. Makes the Bugatti Veyron look like a bargain.

CHINA

Attack of the Clones

Chinese entrepreneurs have been quick to cash in on the booming car business and just like they did with jeans, computer software and DVDs, they've started with a spot of piracy. At auto shows in Shanghai and Beijing, domestic manufacturers have proudly shown 'new' models that bear a striking resemblance to existing models from big-name car-makers. We particularly like the Geely, which looks like an old Citroën ZX, the Chery QQ, which is so obviously a clone of the Chevrolet Spark that GM took legal action, and the JiangLing Landwind, which looks suspiciously like the Honda Passport and scored an astonishing zero stars in crash tests. However, our clear favourite is a Hong Qi (Red Flag) concept from First Automotive, which is an unashamed 'tribute' to the Rolls-Royce Phantom.

Testing Times

With its sudden rush of car ownership, China's road-safety record has plummeted – after all, you couldn't really do much damage on a bicycle. The World Health Organization estimates that 680 people die on China's roads every day. That's *every day*. So, in 2005, the government decided to act by toughening up one of the world's easiest driving tests. Chinese learners now have to demonstrate their skills in a closed compound, complete with a kind of obstacle course, along with a short road drive and theory test. Not that it's likely to have much of an effect on the carnage, as the BBC reported that a driving licence can be bought for around $250, which is the same price as a course of lessons. Guess which is most popular.

Ear We Go

Never mind learning to drive, one Chinese man has come up with a method of car travel that doesn't involve getting behind the wheel. In 2005, 38-year-old Zhang Xingquan from Dehui, Jilin province, pulled a car by his ears for 20 metres – while walking on eggs without breaking any. According to news website Ananova, he learned the trick when he was eight. Guess there wasn't much on TV when he was a kid.

Lucky Numbers

The Chinese are great believers in numerology – how numbers influence life. And this 4000-year-old belief can cause problems for carmakers. Get the number on the boot wrong and nobody will buy the car. Good numbers include 2, 3, 6, 8 and 9, bad ones are 4, 5, 7 and 0, while 1 isn't great, either. Alfa Romeo's 164 would never have sold in Cantonese-speaking regions as the number 4 refers to death and wisely the company changed it to 168 for Malaysia. The number 7 is also associated with death – so the 147 has no hope, either.

INDIA

Taxi Boom

Be very wary of taking an air-conditioned taxi in India. There's anecdotal evidence that more than a few Indian cabbies top up their leaky aircon systems with cheap LPG gas, rather than with expensive refrigerant. It works. The only trouble is that in the event of an accident – hardly a rare occurrence – the cab blows up.

Ambassador for Peace

In 2004, Indian taxi driver Harpreet Devi converted his Hindustan Ambassador taxi to drive in reverse in all four forward gears. His aim was to break the Asian and world records for driving in reverse as well as to drive backwards all the way from the Punjab to Pakistan to help establish peace between India and Pakistan. He told the BBC World Service that driving backwards could prove quite a painful experience. 'I do have pains in the neck – frequent pains in the neck – and I have had severe vomiting in past,' he explained. 'I have got a severe back-bone problem from driving so fast in reverse, because my whole body gets contorted.' But he insisted the pain was worth while. 'To achieve something, you have to do something,' he stressed. 'So it's right that I should be experiencing pain.'

Made in India. Probably not what you expect to hear about the Aston V8 Vantage, but the original concept car was built in Mumbai.

AdVantage India

Mumbai's Dilip Chhabria Design is India's answer to Pininfarina. It was to DC Design that Aston Martin turned to build the V8 Vantage show car – the first time a major car-maker had looked to India for such a job. DC Design also specializes in exotic coachwork for wealthy home-based clients, producing extraordinary one-offs such as a three-door Porsche Cayenne coupé, Rolls-Royce Phantom Coupé and a super-stretched Mercedes S500.

JAPAN

Lost in Translation

Legend has it that the Mitsubishi Starion of the 1980s was supposed to be called the Stallion, and Japanese car names continue to get lost in translation today. Here are ten of our favourites from Japan's car showrooms.

Daihatsu Naked
Honda Fit
Honda Life Dunk
Isuzu Mysterious Utility
Mazda Bongo Friendee
Mazda Laputa
Mazda Scrum
Nissan Cedric
Suzuki Lapin
Toyota Succeed Wagon

The Daihatsu Naked. It'd look an awful lot better with some clothes on.

Queens of the Road

As in most countries, no motor race in Japan is complete without its glamorous grid girls clutching umbrellas and pouting for the cameras. The difference in Japan is that these PVC-clad 'race queens' are probably more popular than the racing itself, attracting legions of obsessed fans – known as 'otaku' – who pay thousands of yen to follow and photograph their queens. Just Google 'race queen' to see what we mean.

Slip, Slidin' Away

The Japanese art of drifting or *dorifto* involves sliding cars sideways through a series of corners, gaining points for style and speed. From its early beginnings in the mountains around Tokyo, *dorifto* has now become a major international motor sport. *Dorifto* has a language all of its own. This should help you understand it.

dorifto	(drifting) Oversteering a car through a corner.
dorikin	(drift king) The name given to Keiichi Tsuchiya – founder of the Dorifto movement.
ikaten	(cool drift heaven) A drifting competition.
tsuiso	(twin-battle drift) A head-to-head competition.
senshu	A competitor.
giri giri	Driving on the edge.
nagareru	(flow) The skill of maintaining a drift corner to corner.
kizu	(wound) Damage sustained during competition.
side dori	A drift initiated by application of the handbrake, also known as e-brake drift.
kansei drift	(also known as inertia drift) A slide induced by sudden weight transfer caused by rapid release of the throttle in a corner.
dirt-drop drift	A sneaky move where the driver actually strays off the tarmac on to the dirt to prolong a powerslide.
feint drift	Momentum-induced drift caused by the driver swerving the opposite way to the approaching corner before aggressively turning-in. Known in rallying circles as the Scandinavian Flick.

| *keri drift* | (also known as the clutch-kick) Depressing the clutch, allowing the engine to rev and then quickly popping the pedal suddenly applies full power to the wheels, causing them to spin and inducing a spectacular, tyre-smoking slide. |

CARtoon Crazy

Japan's obsession with Manga meets motoring in the comic-book series Initial-D. Eighteen-year-old Takumi Fujiwara helps his father Bunta deliver tofu from their home to a hotel near Lake Akina just outside Tokyo. Every day he passes Mount Akina, the birthplace of the *dorifto* phenomenon (see pp. 74–5) and hones his skills. Takumi has been driving since he was 13 and is now an ace behind the wheel. Driving his AE86 Toyota Sprinter Trueno (Corolla Coupé) he takes on all comers to the delight of millions. From its Manga beginnings in 1996 *Initial D* is now a TV anime series, a video game and even a live action movie, while music from the TV show regularly tops the charts in Japan. It's all good, clean fun. Something that can't quite be said about the Viper hentai Manga series. Featuring characters called Mercedes and Carrera, it has nothing to do with cars and plenty to do with more 'traditional' Japanese Manga themes – young girls, well-endowed aliens and the like. Not quite the *Beano*, is it?

Green Fingers

Boffins at Toyota have devised an ingenious way to clean up car pollution. They've developed a new kind of shrub that absorbs nasty substances from the air. The Kirsch Pink is closely related to the Cherry Sage shrub, and Toyota claims that it absorbs nitrogen oxide, sulphur dioxide and other nasties. It also produces lovely pink flowers between May and November.

Decorative Deliveries

Truck drivers in Japan (like many in the Far East) take great pride in adorning their rigs with flamboyant illustrations and decorations. Known as *dekorata*, they're so popular in Japan that several movies and video games have been made starring them. An added bonus is that because the owners have spent so much time, love and money on them, these vehicles are among the most carefully driven in the country.

Hello, Copy Kitty

Japan's fondness for all things foreign and retro can be seen in its craze for turning humdrum domestic micro-cars into, er, humdrum European cars – albeit old ones. Kits can be bought to turn Subaru Sumber vans into old-style VW microbuses (at approximately half-scale). And if that's too mainstream, you can convert your Sumber into a 1950s Citroën van instead, or change Suzuki's Lapin into a Renault 4. Mitsuoka's Viewt has grander ideas. It looks like a MKII Jaguar, but underneath it's a Nissan March (Micra) and therefore probably not much used as a Yakuza getaway car.

Tuneful Trips

Toyota's bB microcar has been billed as a music player on wheels, with nine speakers, 11 different flashing lights and a jack for your iPod. But they needn't have bothered. The Hokkaido Industrial Research Institute has devised a way for the road to play music instead. Special grooves in the road surface boom up a melody through the tyres and into the car as you drive along. The long-term plan is to have different roads sing traditional songs to drivers about the region in which they're driving. A lovely idea. Unless you're a commuter travelling the same road every day, in which case it'll be like 1991 all over again – when you hardly dared drive with the radio on because all you ever heard was 'Love is All Around' by Wet Wet Wet.

NORTH KOREA

Axles of Evil

As part of what President Bush called the 'Axis of Evil', North Korea has a lot to answer for – including the proliferation of god-awful automobiles. After many years of bashing out Mercedes knock-offs, the North Korean car industry entered the 21st century thanks to the Unification Church of Revd Sun Myung Moon – that's the Moonies. Pyonghwa (Peace) Automobiles was set up in 2000 and now makes the Hwiparam (Whistle) and the Ppeokkugi (Cuckoo) based on the Fiat Siena and Doblo.

PAKISTAN

Golf Driver

'Born in Pakistan and proud of it!' That's what the makers of the Sitara City Cart say of the country's first domestically designed and built four-wheel, er, cart. Even without a decent handicap, it's plain to see that this 200cc machine is a golf buggy with headlamps. It seats four, although quite where you'd put your clubs, sorry, luggage is unclear. Options are limited to a flimsy canvas roof, but such luxuries as doors and windows are not included in the $2000 price. Top speed is a claimed 60kmh. But it does have a driving range of 350 km.

TAIWAN

The Truck-tease

In Taiwan, arty trucks are just as popular as in Japan. But the difference is that the *dien tzu hwa che* (electric flashy) trucks provide an additional form of entertainment. They come complete with a stage, flashing lights, a sound system and … strippers. Apparently they're a big hit at weddings, funerals and religious ceremonies.

THAILAND

Bless Me, Father, for I have Crashed

Brahmin priests in Thailand are much in demand after car accidents. Not just to console the victims but also to bless their damaged cars. In a ritual involving flower garlands, candles and holy water, the priests offer protection from future shunts. Much better is to get your car blessed before a crash, or, better still, to consult a priest before you buy – apparently the exact time you bring your new car home can affect its fortune.

Australasia

AUSTRALIA

It's in the Stars

Can your star sign indicate what sort of a driver you are? Don't scoff, because in 2002 Australian financial-services outfit, Suncorp Metway Limited, studied the birth dates of 160,000 accident claimants over a three-year period and came up with a list of policy-holders ranked by their star sign. However, according to a press release dated 10 February 2002, Warren Duke, Suncorp's national manager of personal insurance, said the study was carried out as part of the company's annual review of claims, but there was no intention to use astrology as a rating factor for motor-insurance premiums. Geminis had more accidents than any other sign. He said that Geminis were 'typically described as restless, easily bored and frustrated by things moving slowly'. We know a few Geminis who would dispute this. Nevertheless, here's the star-sign accident-risk list ordered from worst to best.

1. *Gemini (21 May–21 June)*
2. *Taurus (20 April–20 May)*
3. *Pisces (19 February–20 March)*

4. *Virgo (23 August– 22 September)*
5. *Cancer (22 June–22 July)*
6. *Aquarius (20 January–18 February)*
7. *Aries (21 March–19 April)*
8. *Leo (23 July–22 August)*
9. *Libra (23 September–22 October)*
10. *Sagittarius (22 November–21 December)*
11. *Scorpio (23 October–21 November)*
12. *Capricorn (22 December–19 January)*

Bush Trucker Men

Australia's Aboriginal 'bush mechanics' have been keeping cars going since the 1920s, collecting abandoned broken-down motors in the bush, cannibalizing them for spares and getting them going again without the proper tools. Their 'workshop manuals' or *nyurulypa* (good tricks) are kept in the head, and the knowledge and skills are passed from generation to generation by word of mouth and demonstration. Preferred motors are Ford and Holden. Some of the good tricks include brake fluid made from soapy water, welding broken parts using a battery, jumper leads and fencing wire, brake pads carved from mulga-wood using a hatchet, a clutch plate made from bits of a boomerang and windscreen wipers wound from strips of blanket.

Vintage Cars

Australian wine growers said they were seriously thinking of using Chardonnay to power their big Holdens and Falcons in early 2006. Wine prices had fallen and sending their grapes to ethanol distilleries instead of to the wine presses made good business sense, said Granite Belt wine grower Angelo Puglisi. It's not a new idea, in France 100 million litres of wine were converted to ethanol in 2005. And, to think, only a few years ago it was the other way round – using ethanol antifreeze to make wine.

Lovely Rita, Meter Maid

The Meter Maids of Surfers Paradise on the Gold Coast don't dish out tickets, they actually feed the meters of tourists so they don't get fined. Dressed only in the skimpiest gold-Lycra bikinis they've been a feature of the beaches since 1965, saving thousands from court cases and offering eye candy for millions. Nice work, sheilas.

Location, Location, Location

A canny property developer in Sydney offered a free microcar with trendy Docklands apartments in 2005. Flat buyers would get the Smart For Two for nothing as long as they bought a $25,000 parking space to go with it. The space offered was half that of a normal car park, but the 2.5-metre Smart slotted in neatly.

NEW ZEALAND

The Flying Kiwi

Hiroshi Kumano drove for 500 miles from Tauranga to Twizel, New Zealand, in a Renault with no brakes before being stopped by police. The drive included 230 miles on a busy state highway and 210 miles on a twisty road with many steep gradients. Police said that his swerving between lanes, steering into kerbs and verges and crunching of gears to reduce speed made him New Zealand's most irresponsible driver. Maybe, but he had a few admirers who reckoned that only a Kiwi with supreme skill could have completed the no-brakes drive without major incident.

Feel the Afterburn

Kiwi loony Bruce Simpson has created the world's first pulse-jet powered go-kart. The New Zealand inventor has been 'tinkering with pulse-jet technology' since 1999 and claims to be able to build an engine with 150 lbs of thrust for less than $1000. It was natural, then, that he should bolt it to a home-made kart in 2003 and hurtle down the road at speeds up to 60mph. But that wasn't enough, so Bruce fitted two of his engines into a slightly bigger frame and created the first pulse-jet dragster in 2005. Oh, and he's made his own cruise missile as well, but it's got him into a spot of bother with the government.

Ninja Rally

A classic car club hired karate experts to act as bodyguards for the cars at its rally in early 2006. The trained assassins were required to protect the cars not from criminals but from birds. The organizers feared that sharp-beaked local keas (a kind of parrot) would scratch valuable bodywork and brought in the karate kids to scare them away.

ANTARCTICA

Antarcticars

With temperatures dropping as low as −130°F (−90°C), it's hardly the most hospitable place for an afternoon's drive, but several explorers have actually taken cars to the Antarctic. Back in 1907, Shackleton (the Commander of the British Antarctic Expedition) took an Arrol-Johnston 12–15hp four-cylinder with skis fitted under the front wheels. As *Autocar* reported on 19 October 1907: 'Shackleton has provided himself with a real live motor car with which he hopes to reach his goal and hoist the Union Jack.' Obviously, it was useless and kept getting stuck. In 1927, Sir Hubert Wilkins headed south with an Austin Seven, while in 1963 the Australian National Antarctic Research Expedition commandeered a VW Beetle. Herbie clearly had gone bananas.

FOUR

Pop Idle

We drum our fingers on the steering wheel, sing tunelessly where no-one can hear and annoy the neighbourhood at 120 decibels. Our radios, CDs and iPods are as vital a component in our cars as the wheels and the engine. Music and motor cars have gone together since the dawn of driving. Cars and roads have inspired bands and songwriters from The Beach Boys to the 504 Boyz. Cars have made music – quite literally in some cases – not just as the subjects of songs but even as the substance of the instruments too.

The Mazda Tribute

The earliest car song is believed to be Guy Edwards's 1905 ditty 'In My Merry Oldsmobile' and the airwaves have been jammed with tributes to the automobile ever since. But it always seems to be the fancy cars that get the attention – from Prince's 'Little Red Corvette' to Janis Joplin's 'Mercedes-Benz' or Springsteen's 'Pink Cadillac'. What about the, er, 'unsung' heroes of the motor world, the humdrum cars – don't they deserve a tune or two? Well, yes, they do, and here they are:

Car: Citroën DS21
Song: 'DS21'
Artist: Jane Child
The electro-pop songstress's story told of one girl's love affair with a hydro-pneumatic classic.

The Citroën DS21: loved by French diplomats and English pop princesses alike.

Car: Ford Cortina
Song: 'Grey Cortina'
Artist: Tom Robinson Band
Tom Robinson's tribute to a boy racer's dream machine.

Car: 1983 Mazda coupé
Song: 'Metallic Mazda'
Artist: Lano Places
Norwegian indie band Lano Places tell the tale of another car-obsessed girl and how horsepower is the way to her heart.

Car: A Suzuki
Song: 'New Suzuki'
Artist: Beenie Man
The reggae superstar can afford a supercar, but instead scores in a Suzuki.

Car: Vauxhall Velox
Song: 'From a Vauxhall Velox'
Artist: Billy Bragg
The Bard of Barking's tale of love in the back – she asked if the seats folded down and he told her to pull the handle.

Car: A Volvo
Song: 'Volvo Driving Soccer Mom'
Artist: Everclear
American indie freaks Everclear relate the transformation of a once wild child into the queen of the suburbs.

Who's gonna drive you home?

Cars haven't just inspired songs; they've inspired bands. Here's our top ten – of course we really wanted to include some Motown, but the closest we came was Booker T. and the MGs but sadly it stands for Memphis Group not Morris Garages.

1. *The Cars* *Boston-based New Wavers who, appropriately, are best known for* 'Drive'.

2. *The Datsuns* *New Zealand rockers known for* 'Supergyration' *which is something most Datsuns did at about 75mph.*

3. *The Edsels* *American doo-whoppers whose* 'Rama Lama Ding Dong' *was rather more successful than the Ford they named themselves after.*

4. **Trabant** *Ambient electronic Icelanders. Their* 'Moment of Truth' *was also experienced by Trabby owners on every journey.*

5. **Polski Fiat** *Also from Boston, Massachusetts, offering a bizarre mix of guitars and electronics that's a lot faster than their namesake.*

6. **Jeep** *The former drummer with US band The Samples is out on his own. Still somewhat in the wilderness.*

7. **Cadillac Tramps** *California punk rockers, definitely not Fleetwood Mac.*

8. **Hey Mercedes** *Heavy on the guitars, this midwestern band's* 'Quality Revenge at Last' *could just as easily apply to the German car firm.*

9. **Big Block Dodge** *Hailing from North Carolina, BBD play what they call 'groosion' on their album* Manifold Destiny. *It's exhausting.*

10. **DJ Honda** *Japanese hip-hop star and something of a legend.*

'Oh Lord, Won't You Buy Me a Mercedes-Benz?'

Janis Joplin started it all with these immortal words, 'Oh Lord, won't you buy me a Mercedes-Benz? / My friends all drive Porsches, I must make amends'. Thirty years later and a Benz is obligatory in certain music circles. When it comes to bling, a Mercedes is a must-have and no self-respecting gangsta can seem to write a song without mentioning a Merc. We found more than 200 tracks where a Benz is brought up – mostly by 50 Cent ('21 Questions', 'In Da Hood', 'Poor Lil' Rich Nigga', 'P.I.M.P.', 'Elementary', 'Wanksta', 'Get Rich or Die Tryin'' etc., etc.) but also Pink ('Get the Party Started'), DJ Jazzy Jeff and the Fresh Prince ('Summertime'), 2Pac ('Picture Me Rollin'), Missy

Elliot ('Go to the Floor') and Lil' Romeo ('Your ABCs'). By contrast we could barely reach double figures for BMW, and even Cadillac mustered only 100 mentions.

Beach Buggies

When they weren't singing about surf or crooning over 'California Girls', The Beach Boys were probably the most prolific car songwriters of all time. These are the hot-rodders' automotive anthems: 'Car Crazy Cutie', 'Cherry Cherry Coupé', 'Custom Machine', 'Drive-In', 'Fun Fun Fun', 'Honkin' Down the Highway', 'In My Car', 'In the Parkin' Lot', 'Little Deuce Coupé', 'Little Honda' (OK, so it's about a bike), 'Our Car Club', 'Shut Down', 'Spirit of America', 'Still Cruisin'' and 'This Car of Mine'.

The King of Cadillacs

For the King of rock 'n' roll there was only one car that counted – the Cadillac. Actually, Elvis Presley owned around 30 of them, and there are an estimated 90 more that he gave away to friends and family over a 20-year period. The King bought his first Cad (he never called them Caddys) in March 1955 – a pink and white 1954 model – and, although it caught fire in June that year, it started a love affair that would last until the very end. Of all the Cads the King owned, a 1955 Fleetwood 60 Special was the closest to his heart. Bought for his mother and painted pink and white, it was the only car he kept throughout his life. A 1968 Eldorado Coupé didn't receive such good treatment – Elvis shot it in the right front fender when it wouldn't start. The most Elvis ever spent on one car was $100,000 on a 1960 Series 75 Fleetwood Limousine, customized by George Barris (creator of TV's Batmobile, among others). The car was lavishly laden with gold inside and featured a phone, shoe buffer, fridge and a ten-record automatic RCA record player, a TV and a tape deck. The hubcaps, wheel covers, headlight rims and the grille were plated in 24-carat gold. Barris and Elvis teamed up again to create the Elvis Dream

Cadillac based on a 1965 Eldorado Convertible that was valued at $250,000 when it was finally completed in 1986, nine years after his death. Again, gold was a key feature with no less than 40 coats of gold pearl paint on the exterior, plus a gold-plated steering wheel, gold-plated TV and phone together with three gold Elvis 45s and guitar-shape sun visors to finish it off. Elvis once spent $140,000 on Cadillacs in a single day, buying 14 cars from Madison Cadillac on 27 July 1975. It's hardly a surprise, then, that for his final journey the King's transportation was a 1977 Miller-Meteor Landau Traditional Cadillac hearse, followed by procession comprising one silver Cadillac limousine and 16 more white ones, all Cadillacs of course.

Rock 'n' Rollers

Rock and Rolls-Royces are inextricably linked. Rumours that The Who's Keith Moon drove his Rolls into a swimming pool may be unfounded, but truth never got in the way of a good rock-'n'-roll legend. John Lennon added to the Roller's rock-cred by having his 1965 Phantom V custom painted in psychedelic colours by a group of artists who normally decorated gypsy caravans and canal boats. Other modifications included a rear seat that converted into a double bed, a telephone, television and fridge. The Rolls was also fitted with a loud-hailer. The Beatles used the car regularly from 1966 to 1969, but in 1970 John shipped the Phantom to the USA. It spent several years in storage before being donated to New York's Cooper-Hewitt National Design Museum, part of the Smithsonian Institute, in return for a $225,000 tax credit (John and Yoko had been having some troubles with the Internal Revenue Service). In 1985 the car was auctioned by Sotheby's and fetched an alarming $2.3 million – almost ten times the estimate. It currently resides in The Bristol Motors workshop in Victoria, Canada, where it is being gently restored. The latest Phantom has also scored a series of hits, becoming the hottest car in the 'hood. Hip-hop big-shot owners include 50 Cent, Sean 'Puffy' Coombes, Reverend Run, Nelly and Missy Elliot. Bling bling.

'Baby, you can drive my car': something John Lennon never said to Yoko after he bought this Roller.

Slave to the Rhythm

Listening to fast music can make drivers put the pedal to the metal and increase the chances of crashing. A study by Israeli researchers in 2002 found that the faster the music, the faster the driver went. Tests on a driving simulator at the Ben-Gurion University also showed that drivers listening to up-tempo music were twice as likely to run a red light. Another study in Canada in 2004 found that listening at high volume can seriously hamper your ability to drive. Reaction times were up to 20 per cent slower when music was played at 95 decibels, compared to listening at a less ear-bashing 53 decibels. So if you want to stay safe you'll need a nice gentle bit of Phil Collins – although sheer boredom might force you deliberately to drive off the road ...

Dancing Horses

'Do you own a Ferrari? / Do you live in a wonderful place with a smile on your face?' So sang soft rocker Chris Rea on his album *La Passione*. Rea is such a Ferrari fan that he not only wrote the song but also made a movie about the 1961 156 Sharknose Ferrari racing car driven by Wolfgang von Tripps – even going so far as having a perfect replica of the car constructed. Pink Floyd drummer Nick Mason is also a devoted follower, owning among others an F40, a 250 GTO, a 512S and Gilles Villeneuve's 1978 F1 car. Soul legend Sam Cooke left his Ferrari idling outside the motel where he was shot dead in 1964, and Elvis Presley also left a Dino 308 GT4 behind when he died. As for today's chart-topping Tifosi – take a look at this top ten, in order of performance (cars, not record sales).

1. Jay Kay – Enzo
2. Rod Stewart – Enzo
3. Michael Jackson – F430
4. Robbie Williams – 360 Modena
5. Britney Spears – 360 Modena Spider
   (bought for husband Kevin Federline)
6. LL Cool J – 360 Modena Spider
7. P Diddy – 360 Modena Spider
8. Master P – 360 Modena
9. Wyclef Jean – 360 Modena Spider
10. Dr Dre – 360 Modena Spider

Ode to a Road

Synthesizer wizards Kraftwerk created a whole new genre of music when they released 'Autobahn' in 1975 – a slightly spooky and very lengthy instrumental journey down the unlimited roads of Germany. In 1977, the Tom Robinson Band offered a similar tribute to fast-moving traffic with '2-4-6-8 Motorway'. There are, however, a number of very

A Ferrari racing car and Shirley Bassey together on a stage was Chris Rea's dream come true. And a nightmare for movie-goers.

If you're listening to 'King of the Ring' when you're driving the Nürburgring circuit you'll need to play play it Lauda.

specific odes to roads. Here are our favourites – roads that is – which is why you won't find Chris Rea's *The Road to Hell* on our list. It's about the M25.

Nürburgring
Where does it go? Er, around in a big circle – it's the world's scariest race-track, round the village of Nürburg in the Eifel mountains of Germany
Song: 'King of the Ring'
Artist: Ray Garvey

Route 66
Where does it go? Across America from Chicago to Los Angeles
Song: 'Route 66'
Artists: Chuck Berry, Nat 'King' Cole, The Rolling Stones, Depeche Mode and many others have got their kicks motoring west along this one

A303
Where does it go? From Popham, Hampshire (M3, junction 8) to Honiton, Devon, via Stonehenge
Song: '303'
Artist: Kula Shaker

Highway 51
Where does it go? From northern Wisconsin to New Orleans, Louisiana
Song: 'Highway 51'
Artist: Bob Dylan

Pacific Coast Highway
Where does it go? Down the California coast from Fort Bragg, north of San Francisco, to San Juan Capistrano, south of Los Angeles
Song: 'Pacific Coast Highway'
Artist: Sonic Youth

Rap your Ride

American hip-hop stars are well known for their wars of words, and they've also moved into wars of wheels – competing for the honour of the 'illest rides' in car competitions. Former MC Funkmaster Flex has turned to full-time car customizing and not only builds cars for the stars including 50 Cent, Busta Rhymes and Missy Elliot but also runs a touring celebrity car show and hosts his own MTV programme *Ride with Funkmaster Flex*. Flex has even teamed up with Ford to create tricked-up versions of its Fusion and F-150 pick up truck. Meanwhile, Master P from 504 Boyz has his own line of custom rims (wheels), and Wyclef Jean, who has spent a reported $3 million on a fleet of cars, hopes to go one better by launching his own sports car. It's apparently a cross between a Ferrari and a Corvette but will be 'affordable'. With 20-inch diamond-encrusted wheels as an extra of course.

Mr Milbrodt's Honda Car Parts Band

For some, the simple sound of an engine on song is music enough, but New Jersey-based composer Bill Milbrodt decided he could go one better and created a whole orchestra of instruments from his old Honda Accord. When the car came to the end of its useful life in 1994, Milbrodt had a team of mechanics strip it down to its component parts and then joined forces with local metal sculptor Ray Faunce III to build his band. The Car Music Project comprises the 'tank bass' (made from the petrol tank and part of the radiator), 'air guitar' (made from the air cleaner and part of the windscreen support), 'strutbone' (built from one of the McPherson suspension struts), 'tube flute' (from an air-conditioning tube), 'trunk drum' (from the boot lid), 'exhausto-phone' (from the exhaust system) and a 'percarsion' set that includes gears, springs, windows, wheel drums and cymbals made from the car's floor. Milbrodt's five-piece band plays regularly at arts festivals all over the United States.

Bill Milbrodt, his band and the instruments they made from an old Honda. No accordion, though.

Road to Hell

If you don't blow your own brains out, overdose on drugs or meet your maker in an aircraft accident, a car crash is still a sure-fire way to end up in the rock-'n'-roll hall of fame.

Marc Bolan, the '20th-century Boy', died when his wife, Gloria Jones, crashed their car into a tree on 16 September 1977.

Eddie Cochran took his own 'three steps to heaven' when the car he was in blew a tyre and crashed into a lamp post en route to London Airport on 17 April 1960.

Falco, the 'Rock Me Amadeus' singer, died on 6 February 1998 in a head-on collision with a bus while on holiday in the Dominican Republic.

Jerome Smith of KC & The Sunshine Band had to 'give it up' on 28 July 2000, when he was crushed to death by a bulldozer after accidentally falling off it.

Lisa 'Left-Eye' Lopes of TLC was killed in a high-speed crash in Honduras on 26 April 2002.

Andy McVann of The Farm 'bought the farm' when he lost control of his car during a high-speed police chase on 1 October 1986.

Rushton Moreve of Steppenwolf was 'born to be wild' but killed in a car crash on 1 July 1981.

Cozy Powell of Black Sabbath got the 'kiss of death' in his Saab 9000 when he crashed on the M4 doing in excess of 100mph on 7 April 1998.

Dave Prater of Sam and Dave said 'goodnight, baby' when he was killed in a car accident on the way to visit his mother in Georgia on 9 April 1988.

B. J. Wilson of Procol Harum went 'a whiter shade of pale' and died on 8 October 1990 after months in a coma following a car accident.

FIVE

Screen Machines

No action movie is complete without a car chase. We look on in disbelief as the car drives, full-throttle, into oncoming traffic before leaping over an impossible obstacle, launching it clear of its pursuers and into iconic status. Car movies, TV shows and video games allow us to indulge our wildest automotive fantasies, and that's why we love them. Join us, as we celebrate cars on celluloid, on screen and in silicon.

Silver-Screen Machines

'I get around as nature intended – in a car,' says Kate (Meg Ryan) in the 1995 movie *French Kiss*. And with that classic line, we kick off our big-screen celebration.

Movie Reviews

Why should Jeremy Clarkson be your only onscreen adviser when it comes to cars? The movies are full of handy road tests if you listen closely enough. Woody Allen, John Travolta, Scarlett Johansson – they're all after Clarkson's job.

Bentley
Movie: *Manhattan Murder Mystery* (1993)
Reviewer: Larry Lipton (Woody Allen)
Verdict: 'I always think a Bentley is in good taste.'

Chevrolet Corvette

Movie: *True Lies* (1994)

Reviewer: Simon (Bill Paxton)

Verdict: 'The 'Vette gets 'em wet.'

Chevrolet Nova

Movie: *The Toxic Avenger Part III: The Last Temptation of Toxie* (1989)

Reviewer: Claire (Phoebe Legere)

Verdict: 'I don't mind being blind: I'll never have to see ugliness, or poverty, or pollution, or the Chevrolet Nova.'

Dodge Monaco

Movie: *The Blues Brothers* (1980)

Reviewer: Officer Mount (Steven Williams)

Verdict: 'I don't believe it. It's that shitbox Dodge again!'

Honda Insight

Movie: *Be Cool* (2005)

Reviewer: Chilli Palmer (John Travolta)

Verdict: 'It's the Cadillac of hybrids.'

Oldsmobile Silhouette

Movie: *Get Shorty* (1995)

Reviewer: Chilli Palmer (John Travolta)

Verdict: 'It's the Cadillac of minivans.'

Pontiac Firebird

Movie: *American Beauty* (1999)

Reviewer: Lester Burnham (Kevin Spacey)

Verdict: '1970 Pontiac Firebird. The car I always wanted and now I have it. I rule!'

Porsche

Movie: *Lost in Translation* (2003)

Reviewer: Charlotte (Scarlett Johannson)

Verdict: 'You're probably just having a mid-life crisis. Did you buy a Porsche yet?'

Rolls-Royce

Movie: *Mrs Winterbourne* (1996)

Reviewers: Connie and Paco (Ricki Lake and Miguel Sandoval)

Verdict: Connie – 'Wow, that's like the Cadillac of automobiles, huh?' Paco – 'No, the Mercedes-Benz is the Cadillac of automobiles. This is a Rolls-Royce.'

The Hyundai Matrix

OK, so the Hyundai Matrix wasn't actually named after the blockbuster movie, although such is the car's sluggish pace that driving it feels like you're experiencing the film's trademark bullet time. However, there are a number of cars that only became publicly available after first appearing on the big screen.

The Road Runner of 1968 appeared after Plymouth paid a reported $50,000 to license the name and image of the famous cartoon bird for its muscle car. Steve McQueen's 1968 *Bullitt* Mustang Fastback is one of the most famous movie cars in the world, yet it took until 2002 for Ford to cash in with the launch of the Bullitt Mustang. The limited run of 6500 cars featured uprated running gear based on the SVT Cobra. In 1981, Citroën joined the movie-merchandizing game with a run of 500 yellow 2CVs – replicas of the car featured in *For Your Eyes Only*. The cars came complete with 007 logos on the doors and bonnet and even a series of bullet holes. In 2001, Land-Rover released a Tomb Raider limited-edition (LE) version of its Defender. The Tomb Raider LE boasted Bonatti grey paint, a hefty roofrack and a row of spotlights. Sadly, no Angelina Jolie in the passenger seat, though.

Dr Know?

James Bond is well known for his Aston Martins, his Lotus Esprits and his rather dubious period of driving assorted BMWs, but 007 has helmed a number of rather less highly publicized vehicles as well:

Alfa-Romeo
Bond steals a GTV6 from a woman using a payphone in *Octopussy*.

AMC
007 pinches an AMC Hornet Sportabout in *The Man with the Golden Gun* and goes on to perform one of the greatest car stunts ever (see The Stunt with the Golden Computer, p. 103).

Audi
In *The Living Daylights*, Bond drives two Audi 200 quattros (one saloon and one Avant).

Bentley
Ian Fleming originally had Bond in a Bentley, and he's featured behind the wheel of a Blower three times – in *From Russia with Love*, *Casino Royale* and *Never Say Never Again*.

Citroën
After the anti-theft device on Bond's Lotus is triggered the car explodes, and he has to join Melina Havelock in her Citroën 2CV in *For Your Eyes Only*.

Ford
Bond had his *Bullitt* moment driving a Mustang Mach One through Las Vegas in *Diamonds Are Forever* and spent some time behind the wheel of a classic Fairlane in *Die Another Day* as part of Ford's all-encompassing product placement.

Filming The Living Daylights *with Timothy Dalton and an Audi 200, two very short-lived stars of the Bond franchise.*

Land-Rover
Bond drives a military-spec Defender in Gibraltar the opening sequence of *The Living Daylights*.

Mercedes
007 turns a Mercedes 250SE into a train, chasing baddies down the railway tracks in *Octopussy*.

Renault
Giving chase to May Day (played by Grace Jones), Bond commandeers a Renault 11 taxi in *A View to a Kill* – actually better make that half a Renault 11 taxi.

Toyota

In *You Only Live Twice* Bond pinches a rare 2000GT convertible from a showroom. He should have kept it – only two were made.

The Stunt with the Golden Computer

The amazing spiralling jump that James Bond pulls off in his AMC Hornet in *The Man with the Golden Gun* was originally considered impossible. But thanks to a UNIVAC (UNIVersal Automatic Computer) and the Calspan Corporation the stunt was proved feasible in a simulation. Using their Highway Object Vehicle Simulation Model software Calspan showed the jump *would* work and even recommended some minor suspension modifications to ensure a perfect landing. The modifications were as good as gold and the stunt was filmed in one take.

Hooray for Hybrids

The hottest car in Hollywood is not a flashy Phantom but a humble hybrid. The Toyota Prius is the must-have motor for Tinseltown's eco-conscious stars of the silver screen. The car has become such a success that it even attracted the attentions of America's King of Kustom George Barris (see The Barrismobile, p. 114). The Barris Prius, commissioned by the *New York Times*, had $10,000 of bodywork sculpting, tangerine orange metallic paintwork and special 18-inch wheels.

Stars in Hybrid Cars

Alexandra Paul, Alicia Silverstone, Billy Crystal, Brad Pitt, Cameron Diaz, David Duchovny, Ellen DeGeneres, Harrison Ford, Jack Black, Jack Nicholson, Kevin Bacon, Kirk Douglas, Kurt Russell, Leonardo DiCaprio, Patricia Arquette, Rob Reiner, Robin Williams, Salma Hayak, Susan Sarandon, Steven Spielberg, Tim Robbins, Ted Danson, Tom Hanks, Woody Harrelson and Will Ferrell.

George Gets Tango'd

George Clooney has shunned the popular Prius in favour of the super-fast, supergreen Tango electric car. Designed by the Commuter Car Corporation and built by British motorsport experts Prodrive, the $80,000 single-seater city car, can scorch 0–60 in just four seconds. Range is only 80 miles, but gorgeous George can always top the charge up at his luxury trailer on set.

The Fastest Moustache in the Movies

Think road movie and just one man (and one moustache) springs to mind – Burt Reynolds. In the 1970s and 1980s if you saw a car chase at the cinema there was every chance that Reynolds would be in the driving seat. From cop to robber, moonshiner to motor racer, Burt has played them all.

The Dukes of Hazzard (2005)
Burt plays: The Duke boys' nemesis, Boss Hogg
Burt drives: Mid-70s white Cadillac Eldorado, complete with cow horns

Gumball 3000 The Movie (2003)
Burt plays: The narrator
Burt drives: He doesn't

Driven (2001)
Burt plays: Indy race-team owner Carl Henry
Burt drives: A wheelchair

Cannonball Run II (1983)
Burt plays: Has-been racer J. J. McClure
Burt drives: Chrysler Imperial

Smokey & the Bandit III (1983)
Burt plays: Bootlegging Bandit Bo Darville
Burt drives: 1982 Pontiac Trans Am

Stroker Ace (1983)
Burt plays: NASCAR racer Stroker Ace
Burt drives: NASCAR 'Chicken Pit' Thunderbird

The Cannonball Run (1980)
Burt plays: Has-been racer J. J. McClure
Burt drives: An ambulance

Smokey & the Bandit II (1980)
Burt plays: Bootlegging Bandit Bo Darville
Burt drives: Pontiac Trans Am Turbo

Hooper (1978)
Burt plays: Stuntman Sonny Hooper
Burt drives: A rocket-powered Trans Am (among others)

Smokey & the Bandit (1977)
Burt plays: Bootlegging Bandit Bo Darville
Burt drives: Pontiac Trans Am

WW and the Dixie Dancekings (1975)
Burt plays: Armed robber W. W. Bright
Burt drives: 1955 Oldsmobile

White Lightning (1973)
Burt plays: Ex-con-turned-federal-snitch Gator McKlusky
Burt drives: Souped-up Ford LTD sedan

The Bullitt Bug

From the moment the two goons in the black Dodge Charger R/T first buckle up and smoke their tyres to the time when Frank Bullitt in his green Mustang Fastback forces them off the road into an instant cremation at a petrol station, the two cars pass the same dark-green VW Beetle no less than four times. Other continuity gaffes in this legendary movie include clearly being able to see the Charger reappear behind the petrol station as it explodes and the same car losing a total of five hubcaps during the chase. But it's still one of the best, most authentic, car chases ever captured on film.

Goldfender

It's the *Most Famous Car in the World* according to a 1992 book about Bond's car by David Worrell. And since it's estimated that more than two billion people have watched a James Bond movie, he's probably right. But now, Bond's Aston Martin DB5 isn't just the most well-known movie car – it's the most expensive. At an auction in Phoenix, Arizona, in January 2006, the 1965 DB5, complete with ejector seat, Browning machine guns, tyre-slashing wheels, oil-slick nozzles and retractable bullet-proof screen, was bought for $2,090,000. The buyer was an un-named European collector. With a fluffy white cat and plans for world domination, no doubt.

The OsCARS

Car pictures haven't exactly swept the boards at the annual Academy Awards, but as you can see below there are a few motor movies that have picked up an OsCAR or two:

Speed (1994) Sound and Sound Effects Editing
Driving Miss Daisy (1989) Best Picture, Actress (Jessica Tandy),
    Makeup, Screenplay

Motor Mania

The French Connection *(1971) Best Picture, Actor (Gene Hackman),*
  Director (William Friedkin), Film Editing, Screenplay
Bullitt *(1968) Film Editing*
Grand Prix *(1966) Film Editing, Sound, Sound Effects*
The Great Race *(1965) Sound Effects*
Thunderball *(1965) Special Visual Effects*
Goldfinger *(1964) Sound Effects*
It's a Mad Mad Mad Mad World *(1963) Sound Effects*

Crash 'n' burn

Picking the best car movie of all time is, frankly, just too difficult.
Instead we thought we'd look at the worst. And with the help of the
Annual Golden Raspberry (RAZZIE) Award we have a conclusive bottom-
five car movies of all time. You might notice they've got something in
common – a certain moustachioed actor. Yes, poor old Burt has a total
of seven Razzie nominations and one win. We're sure he'd have got
more, but the awards only began in 1980:

The Dukes of Hazzard *(2005) Eight nominations, including Worst*
  Picture (no wins)
Cannonball Run II *(1983) Eight nominations, including Worst*
  Picture (no wins)
Driven *(2001) Seven nominations, including Worst Picture (no wins)*
Stroker Ace *(1983) Five nominations, including Worst Picture*
  (one winner: Worst Supporting Actor – Jim Nabors)
The Cannonball Run *(1980) One nomination (Farrah Fawcett –*
  Worst Supporting Actress)

Method in the Madness

Robert De Niro is well-known for his method acting. De Niro likes to
become the character he plays, really to absorb himself in the part.
But during the filming of *Ronin* he didn't need to act at all. For the

film's sensational chase on the Périphérique of Paris, De Niro has to race after Jonathan Pryce and Natascha McElhone in their BMW into oncoming traffic at 75mph. Stunt coordinator Jean-Claude Lagniez had De Niro's Peugeot modified with a set of controls on the right so that he could drive and De Niro could hold a dummy steering wheel and act. But during rehearsals De Niro was nervous. So in jumped director John Frankenheimer and told Lagniez to drive at full speed. Then he got his wife to join him in the car. 'You see, Bob,' said Frankenheimer, 'if she did it, you can do it.' De Niro agreed but the resulting shots clearly show that he was seriously scared by the scene. So much for the tough-guy image, Bob.

The Driver

Former French rallycross champion Rémy Julienne is probably the world's most prolific and talented stunt driver. With more than 120 movies to his credit in his 40-year career, including six James Bond films, Julienne is still best known for his work on *The Italian Job*. Julienne drove Mini Coopers down stairs, through a shopping centre, down sewers and over the rooftops of Turin and set a whole new standard for car chases. He even devised a special stunt show for Disneyland, involving reverse jumps and balletic spins.

Stars in Fast Cars

When you think about Hollywood heroes who have taken to the track, the names McQueen, Newman and Dean are usually first on the grid. But what about Diaz, Eastwood and Shatner – they've all raced cars, with varying degrees of success, at the annual Toyota Pro/Celebrity race at the Grand Prix of Long Beach. Held each April as a support race to the main Champ Car race, the event celebrated its 30th year in 2006. Previous winners include Gene Hackman and Stephen Baldwin, while Cameron Diaz, Patrick Stewart, William Shatner, Clint Eastwood, James Brolin, David Hasselhoff, Woody Harrelson, Cuba

Get your skates on, mate. Frenchman Rémy Julienne tackles The Italian Job *in a very British Mini.*

Gooding Jr, Jason Priestly, Matt Le Blanc, George Lucas and Meatloaf should all stick to acting.

Death Imitates Art

David Cronenberg's controversial *Crash* was pulled from US cinemas in April 1997 after a couple died in what highway safety experts called 'a chilling example of cinema come to life'. *Crash* tells the story of advertising executive James Ballard (James Spader) who, after a near fatal crash, becomes increasingly obsessed with the idea of combining sex and serious car accidents. In one scene Ballard deliberately rams his wife's car off the highway and, in the wreckage, starts to get it on with her (Deborah Unger). Transport Undersecretary Richard Lathon feared *Crash* was being copied when a Ford Aerostar, driven by 25-year-old Chris Gosch and his girlfriend Lisa Bradley, was seen to swerve off a country road and roll over at around 11 p.m. on Saturday, 19 April 1997. Both occupants were killed. The studio pulled the movie from cinemas, and Spader and co-star Rosanna Arquette agreed to star in a TV campaign to promote safe driving.

MTV – Motor Television

They may be on the small screen, but the cars are the big stars in our favourite shows.

Auto Pilot

KITT, the Knight Industries Two Thousand Pontiac Trans Am that partnered David Hasselhoff in *Knight Rider*, could often be seen driving itself. What viewers didn't see (well, only occasionally, if the continuity people missed it) was stuntman Jack Gill disguised inside the car's passenger seat and piloting the car with a set of dual controls. The Hof himself proved to be quite a skilled driver and there were often arguments over who would drive when the two were in the car together.

Hazzardous Waste

'Just good 'ol boys, never meaning no harm' went the theme song. But try telling that to the mechanics who worked on the hit TV show *The Dukes of Hazzard*. During 147 episodes, Bo and Luke totalled over 300 General Lees with their crazed car jumping. Amazingly, out of 1360 American Racing Vector wheels supplied for filming only one ever failed on landing. The General Lee was a 1969 Charger R/T, but after finding original '69 cars hard to come by, the producers were forced to convert a number of 1968 and 1970 models for later episodes. An estimated 17 original General Lees remain today, along with hundreds of replicas, which are proudly displayed at the annual Dukesfest in Nashville, Tennessee. Yee-ha!

BL – The Unprofessionals

The Professionals' heroes Bodie (Martin Shaw) and Doyle (Lewis Collins) are best known for scattering cardboard boxes in their Ford Capri and Escort RS2000. But this dynamic duo actually started out driving a variety of British Leyland cars. In early episodes, the CI5 cops were seen behind the wheel of a Rover P6, Triumph TR7 and Triumph Dolomite Sprint, while boss Cowley (Gordon Jackson) drove an SD1. However, the BL cars were notoriously unreliable (as they were on *The New Avengers*) and production company Mark 1 ditched BL and signed with Ford who provided all the action vehicles including a nice Granada Ghia for Cowley.

Copycat Cops and Robbers

With its huge white stripe and tomato-red paint, the Ford Gran Torino driven by TV cops Dave Starsky (Paul Michael Glaser) and Ken 'Hutch' Hutchinson (David Soul) was probably the least suitable undercover car ever. But it proved so popular with viewers in 1975 that Ford decided to cash in on the craze and released a limited edition of 1000 red Torinos complete with Starsky Stripe. The TV car had a hefty 400-cubic-inch V8, but the Tomato car sold to the public made do with a 351-cubic-inch effort mustering a feeble 138bhp. Hardly enough for a Starsky-style powerslide.

Sixes and Sevens

It took Caterham Cars over 20 years to launch a TV tie-in with the bizarre captive drama *The Prisoner*. In 1990 the company unveiled a special version of the Lotus Seven seen in the show's title sequence driven by 'I am not a number' Patrick McGoohan. When choosing the car for *The Prisoner* in 1967, McGoohan said: 'We needed a car for our hero. Something out of the ordinary. A vehicle to fit his personality … I test-drove it. This was it. A symbol of all *The Prisoner* was

'I am not a number.' Oh, bollocks, I am. I'm a seven.

to represent: standing out from the crowd, quickness and agility, independence, individuality and a touch of the rebel.' Finished in British racing green with a yellow nose, the 47 limited-edition cars came complete with a certificate and dashboard plaque signed by McGoohan himself. As part of the deal McGoohan was given a car – Number Six off the production line, of course.

Viper with no Bite

Following the success of *Knight Rider*, US Network NBC decided to create a new car show around one of the most exciting cars of the 1990s – the Dodge Viper. Set in the 'near future', *Viper* was basically a showcase for Chrysler's range and featured a shiny red 1992 model that morphed into a silver 'Defender' that had an assortment of weaponry, from flame throwers to machine guns. The plot pretty much followed the *Knight Rider* form, with a former getaway driver turned good guy taking on an assortment of baddies. NBC canned the show after one series, but Paramount took it on and made three more series before they saw sense and axed it in 1999.

Real Armani, Fake Ferrari

With his flash suits, pastel T-shirts and no socks, Sonny Crockett (Don Johnson) was cool incarnate in the 1980s smash hit, *Miami Vice*. As an undercover cop infiltrating the seedy Miami underworld, Crockett needed a suitable set of wheels. And what could have been better than his black Ferrari 365GTB/4 Daytona Spyder? Er, a real one perhaps? Crockett's Daytona was in fact a replica, based on a Chevrolet Corvette chassis, and when word got out that it was a fake, both the producers and Ferrari had to respond. For the series' third season, in 1986, Ferrari USA came up with two white Testarossas for Crockett to tool around in. For stuntwork, however, another fake was created, based on an old DeTomaso Pantera chassis and complete with nitrous-oxide injection and an additional footbrake for skids and spins. Ferrari fans will be pleased to know that *Magnum, PI* (Tom Selleck) and *The Persuaders'* Danny Wilde

(Tony Curtis) drove genuine cars – a 308GTS in the case of *Magnum* and a 246 Dino for Danny.

Car-park TV

There's nothing funny about a car park – unless you find the smell of urine, insufficient lighting and the prospect of being mugged amusing. Yet car parks have actually been the subject of two sitcoms. *Mr Aitch* (Harry H. Corbett of *Steptoe & Son* fame) made his screen début on ITV in 1967. With a writing team that had worked on comedy greats including *The Likely Lads*, *Hancock* and *Steptoe* it should have been a success. But grumpy (well, you would be) car-park owner *Mr Aitch* never made it past 15 episodes. ITV tried again in 2000 with *Pay and Display* starring James Bolam and Matt Bardock as two attendants in an underground car park. A traffic warden called Adolf only served to add to the misery and only six half-hour episodes were broadcast.

The Barrismobile

'To the Batmobile, let's go!' It's a cry every young boy looked forward to as the slightly camp, slightly plump Adam West and sidekick Burt Ward would leap into action, fire up the atomic batteries and shoot a jet of flame out of the exhaust. The Batmobile was created in just three weeks by American car-custom legend George Barris, the self-proclaimed 'King of Kustom'. Based on the 1955 Lincoln Futura concept car and powered by a 429-cubic-inch, full race engine, the Batmobile propelled the Dymanic Duo into their adventures and Barris into iconic status. Barris created (and still creates) numerous other classic TV and film cars including the *A-Team* van, the Gran Torino for *Starsky and Hutch*, *The Munsters'* Koach, the General Lee from *The Dukes of Hazzard* and many more. But it's the Batmobile that he'll always be remembered for. All together now: dinner, dinner, dinner, dinner …

Dinner, dinner, dinner, dinner … you know the rest.

Armchair Racers

From their spritely beginnings in the 1970s to the multi-million pound business of the noughties, car-racing video games have become a driving force in entertainment. For 'games', read 'simulators', for nowadays the best of them get astonishingly close to the real thing. So close, in fact, that many racing drivers use them to hone their skills.

Let the Games Begin

Three years after Nolan Bushnell formed Atari and showed the world the very first video game, 1971's *Computer Space*, the first driving game, appeared. *Gran Trak 10* came in the traditional upright video-game cabinet, but with a steering wheel, four-speed gearstick and brake and accelerator pedals. By today's standards *Gran Trak 10*'s graphics (little more than a collection of black and white dots) are laughable, but the game was ground-breaking. The driver was faced with a plan view of a race circuit and had to negotiate his white car around the hairpins without hitting the barriers or slippery oil slicks and rival black cars. It involved plenty of arm-twirling and was the closest that kids in the 1970s ever got to competing in a Grand Prix. Later that year Atari followed it with *Gran Trak 20* – a two-player version with two sets of wheels and pedals. The race to create the ultimate driving game had begun and still continues today.

Coin-op Classics

Before there was a PC, a PS2 or an Xbox in every home, the only place to get your driving kicks as a kid was the arcade. Here are our top-ten coin-ops.

1. **Sega Rally Championship** *(Sega, 1995) Where else can you drift a Lancia Stratos round corners as three mates try to drive you off the road?*

2. **Pole Position** *(Namco, 1985) Race round the Fuji speedway in your Indy car passing checkpoints to get extra time. Simple, but brilliant.*

3. **Outrun** *(Sega, 1986) Actually it was a bit rubbish, but* Miami Vice *was on the telly and this was the closest kids ever got to being Sonny Crockett, driving a Ferrari Testarossa with a hot blonde passenger.*

4. **Super Monaco Grand Prix** *(Sega, 1989) The first real attempt at simulating a race car – you couldn't just plant your foot on the floor and make every turn. That Lowes hairpin is a real bastard.*

5. **Final Lap** *(Namco, 1987) The first two-player linked game, where each driver had his own screen and controls.*

6. **Ridge Racer** *(Namco, 1993) Inspired by the Japanese Midnight Club racers, this was the game that first taught the art of drifting.*

7. **Sega Daytona USA** *(Sega, 1994) Up to eight racers could link up to stage the most spectacular NASCAR pile-ups.*

8. **Chase HQ** *(Taito, 1988) You're a cop and you have to ram the bad guy off the road in your custom Porsche. For the first time crashing is good!*

9. **Virtua Racing** *(Sega, 1992) The most sophisticated simulator of its time, with 3-D graphics, tricky handling and force-feedback steering to add to the driving sensation.*

10. **Sprint 2** *(Atari, 1976) Developed from the original* Gran Trak 10 *it was the grandfather of them all – the first to use a micro-processor.*

Your Home Circuit

The arrival of the home computer and the games console in the 1980s meant millions of kids could now race and chase in their bedrooms on their Ataris, Nintendos, Segas, Sinclairs, Commodores and Colecovisions. But fun though the games were, they were just that – games. But that all changed in 1984 when Geoff Crammond created *Revs* for the BBC Micro. *Revs* was the first real-driving simulator. Your Formula Three race car featured realistic handling, a detailed and accurate Silverstone circuit and was damned near impossible to master with its clunky keyboard controls. Crammond went on to create the award-winning Formula One series of PC games, but he had set the tone for every half-decent race game that followed.

GT - Gigantic Takings

One man who clearly followed Crammond's principles was Kazunori Yamauchi - creator of the world's most successful driving-game franchise. Yamauchi's devotion to realism and attention to detail was first revealed in 1997's *Gran Turismo - The Real Driving Simulator* for the Sony Playstation. Accurate car handling and never-before-seen graphics made it an instant hit. It went on to sell nearly 11 million copies worldwide. *GT2* followed in 1999, *GT3* in 2001, *GT Concept 2001 Tokyo* in 2002, *GT Concept 2002 Geneva* in 2002, *GT4 Prologue* in 2003 and *GT4* in 2004, bringing total worldwide sales to an incredible 44 million by the start of 2006.

Lessons in Laps

Such is the realism of today's driving games that several racing drivers admit to learning race circuits at home on their PS2s or Xboxes. Before 2005's Le Mans 24-hour race, World Rally Champion Sebastien Loeb's sponsors Sony Playstation provided him with a copy of *Gran Turismo 4* to practise the circuit and even built a special simulator for his private plane - probably the only video-game console that's ever had to be airworthiness tested to 9g. 'I had a Playstation simulator in the aircraft so I could learn the track while I travelled,' he said. 'It was invaluable, as I didn't have much time to learn the track. For me, it helped me to learn the corners and the lines.' Before the race he admitted: 'I've spent more time on the game than the real track.'

Before the Shanghai Grand Prix of 2005, Jacques Villeneuve told the *Independent* newspaper that he planned to learn the track on a video game. Villeneuve is a well-known game enthusiast - he even helped develop the 2002 game *Jacques Villeneuve's Racing Vision*. Other drivers to put their names to games include Fernando Alonso, Mario Andretti, Skip Barber, Richard Burns, Bill Elliott, Jeff Gordon, Johnny Herbert, Nigel Mansell, Colin McRae, Richard Petty, Michael Schumacher, Ayrton Senna and Paul Tracy.

SIX

Police! Stop!

Whether you're speeding, stealing or just doing something stupid behind the wheel, the cops are waiting to get you. They've got the technology, they've got the cars and they've got the skills. Well, most of the time, anyway.

Need for Speed

It's not big; it's not clever. But everyone does it. Speeding, that is. Some get caught. Some make excuses. Some get revenge.

Top Speeder

So far we've kept two-wheelers out of this book, but we have to make an exception for Minnesota biker Samuel Armstrong Tilley, as he's the world's fastest-recorded lawbreaker. In September 2004 he was clocked at 205mph on his Honda RC51 motorcycle after being spotted from the air by state-patrol pilot Al Loney. Tilley was riding on US Highway 61 when he throttled up, unaware that he was being timed by the eye in the sky. His exploits topped those of the previous speed-leader, 35-year-old Dr William Faenza from New York, who was nabbed driving his Lamborghini Diablo at 182mph in a 55-mph zone on state road 443 on 31 August 2003.

Daft Radar

But 205mph is nothing to a Belgian and his Mini. Brussels police reportedly issued a ticket to a Mini driver for travelling at 2100mph on the boulevard Lambermont in December 2003. The ticket was retracted after police admitted the radar was probably faulty. In October 2003, South Wales police sent 28-year-old Joanna James a fixed-penalty notice stating that she had been caught on camera doing 480mph in her knackered Austin Maestro.

Easy Meat

Jussi Salonoja, the sausage king of Finland, also holds the honour of receiving the priciest speeding ticket ever issued. After being nabbed driving at 50mph in a 25mph zone the millionaire was fined a record 170,000 euros (£116,000) in February 2004. Finland's fines are income-related and tax-office records showed that Salonoja had earned almost £7 million in 2002. So he could probably afford it.

It Wasn't Me

With the proliferation of speed cameras on the roads, British drivers have become increasingly creative with their excuses for their motoring misdemeanors. Here are our ten favourites from the safety-camera partnerships of Northumbria and Mid- and South Wales.

1. *My ex still has keys to my car and keeps taking it without asking. I haven't reported this to the police.*

2. *My budgie was ill and I was rushing it to the vet.*

3. *I was desperate for the loo and had to speed to the nearest public toilet.*

4. *An ice-scraper fell out of a compartment in the door and jammed under the pedal.*

5. *I picked up a hitchhiker who commented that they liked my car so I let 'this person' drive the vehicle. I don't have their name or address.*

6. *I passed out after seeing UFOs.*

7. *I had a severe bout of diarrhoea.*

8. *A gust of wind pushed me over the limit.*

9. *I was in a hire car and the speedometer was in a different position – I was actually looking at the rev counter by mistake.*

10. *As I entered on to the motorway, my car was dragged along in the slip-stream of a truck. My brakes aren't very good, so I had to keep pace with it.*

Kill your Speed (Camera)

Ever since the speed camera was invented, drivers throughout the world have tried to destroy them. There have been necklacings, chain-saw attacks and shootings, but one Swiss driver did such a thorough job of Gatsocide in November 2005 we have to give him credit. After being snapped at nearly 50mph in a 30mph zone in the Alpine village of La Punt Chamues-ch, the unnamed Swiss assassin got out of his car, grabbed a pickaxe from his boot and smashed the camera down. Then he ran it over and dragged the remains further up the mountain before throwing it down the cliff side. Unfortunately, he was caught in the act by police and arrested for destruction of property. On the plus side, the camera and film were toast, so he probably got off the speeding ticket.

Gotcha! There's no escape from the Gatso camera. But there is always revenge if you're Swiss, own a pickaxe and have a mountain near by.

Cat Nabbed

Police in Malaysia are the sneakiest snappers of all. They use intelligent Cat's-eyes buried in the road to take photographs of speeding cars. The camera-equipped studs buried in the road transmit images to police computers using wireless technology and incorporate number-plate recognition. The studs even clean themselves automatically to ensure a crisp image.

Grand Theft Auto

From spotty teenage joyriders to organized crime bosses, car theft is an epidemic across the world. And as the good guys come up with new ways to protect their cars so the bad guys find new ways to steal them.

Steal the World

One car is stolen every 25 seconds in the USA – that's 1.2 million a year – making it the top joy-riding, car-jacking country in the world (according to the National Insurance Crime Bureau (NICB)). The United Kingdom is Europe's car-crime centre, with close to 400,000 cars pinched every year, with France (300,000) and Italy (260,000) in silver and bronze places (source: Europol). Japan is a pretty safe bet with just 60,000 cars lifted a year (source: Kato Electric), and even the Russians get away lightly with just 70,000 cars nicked (source: Russian Interior Ministry). And despite what many of the following stories would suggest, it's not the most glamorous cars that are targeted by villains, just the old crapsters that you can drive away with a slimjim and a screwdriver.

Stealer's Wheels

Australia *(1994–9)*   *Hyundai Excel (NRMA Insurance)*
USA *(1995)*   *Honda Civic (NICB)*
USA *(1999)*   *Acura Integra (CCC)*
Canada *(2000)*   *Honda Civic SiR (Insurance Bureau of Canada)*
Russia *(since 2002)*   *Chevrolet Niva (Izvestia)*
UK *(2003)*   *Vauxhall Belmont (UK Car Theft Index)*
Hungary   *Trabant (Napi)*
Japan   *Toyota Land Cruiser (Kato Electric)*

Firestarter

In 1997 there were an astonishing 13,000 car-jackings in South Africa. Inventor Charles Fourie decided to get his own back and designed the 'Blaster'. Faced with a car-jack threat, the driver of a Blaster-equipped car presses a button next to the foot pedals. This sets off squirts of liquid gas from nozzles under the car's front doors.

The 2003 Vauxhall Belmont is Britain's most stolen car. The big question is WHY?

The gas clouds are then ignited by an electric spark. The result is a pair of fireballs that barbecue villains on both sides of the car without damaging the paintwork. Apparently it was not illegal to fit a car with the device or actually use it in cases of proven self-defence. South Africans anxious about car-jacking could buy one of Mr Fourie's Blasters in 1999 for the equivalent of $655.

Shocking Fares

Meanwhile, in China the Yantai Qinglu Automation Company has a neat solution for in-taxi robbery and violence. The TPS-4/5 Taxis Protection Cushion sits on the rear seat. If the taxi driver fears imminent violent robbery he or she presses a hidden button and sends a Taser-like 50,000 pulsating volts into the cushion. This, in the same way as the Taser used by police forces worldwide, will instantly disable the passenger without doing any permanent damage.

One Finger One Thumb Keep Moving

Car-jackers in Kuala Lumpur, Malaysia, were initially baffled by their victim's car-security system in March 2005. The biometric device required the driver's fingerprint to be scanned before the car could be driven. But the villains soon figured out a solution. They chopped off the driver's finger and sped off.

Better Late than Never

New Yorker Alan Poster was distraught when his blue 1968 Chevrolet Corvette was stolen from a garage. He didn't have theft insurance and couldn't replace it. But, fortunately, the car was returned after it was discovered by US customs officials in a shipping container in California, having been sold to a Swedish buyer. The car was now silver, but so was Poster – it was 37 years since the theft.

Gone Wrong in 60 Seconds

A gang of thieves in Manteca, California, pulled off a cinematic-style heist when they pinched a $165,000 Ford GT in December 2005. The crew broke into Manteca Ford at 4 a.m. and smashed into a key safe. The GT had a flat battery, so they boosted it with a charger, then rolled a Mustang belonging to rapper 50 Cent out of the way and drove out through the showroom's plate-glass window. The villains then grabbed a Lincoln Navigator to ram through the dealership's gates before tearing off in the GT. The robbery could almost have been a scene from *Gone in 60 Seconds*, if it weren't for one thing. Having done all the hard work, the gang crashed the 200mph GT just down the road and legged it.

Despite careful planning, the first boost of a Ford GT went Pete Tong when thieves crashed the 200mph car just yards from the showroom. Muppets.

Fraud Fiesta

There are so many tests, rules and regulations related to road use that it's no wonder the scammers are busy abusing the system.

Exam Scam

Toyota was caught helping thousands of staff to cheat in a mechanics exam in 2003. The world's number-two car-maker was asked by Japan's transport ministry to help devise some of the questions in the test and the answers were 'leaked' on to an internal website. Of the 7300 candidates taking the test, almost half were from Toyota dealers and most had looked at the website.

Dummy Run

Greg Pringle from Colorado was busted for driving in a 'high occupancy vehicle' lane in January 2006. The lane is reserved for cars carrying two or more people, but Pringle's passenger was not all he seemed. 'He' was a shop-window mannequin dressed in a grey sweatshirt and baseball cap. Still, at least his passenger couldn't tell him, 'I told you so.'

Buried Beemer

Ohio man Matthew Mueller couldn't afford to repair the blown engine of his BMW in 2002, so he hired a digger, buried the car on his father's farm and reported it stolen. The insurers paid up $20,000 and Mueller got a new car. But three years later police were tipped off to his scam, dug up the car and Mueller was banged up for a year for fraud.

Indian Dope Trick

Ramar Pillai, a self-taught scientist, was doing a roaring trade selling herbal fuel in Madras, India, before being arrested for fraud in 2000. Pillai claimed his fuel was made from a variety of Indian herbs but refused to reveal his secret recipe, which he sold at 11 fuel stations. That's probably because his fuel was in fact a mixture of benzene and toluene with no evidence of any herbs at all.

Repo Reptiles

When the ABSA bank of Johannesburg, South Africa, repossessed Abel Manamel's car he exacted a reptilian revenge in January 2004. Manamel walked into a branch and demanded his car be returned before releasing several venomous snakes from his bag. 'I had ten puff adders, three mambas and another two cobras,' he said. One bank worker was bitten in the ensuing chaos. A warrant for attempted murder was issued, and Manamel never did get his car back.

Dumb & Dumber

When they engage Drive, plenty of people appear to disengage Brain.

Businessman or Boy Racer?

New Zealand businessman John Rae had his Mercedes CLS impounded in January 2006 after doing a burnout in front of a police car – with his wife and mother-in-law on board. Rae was charged under anti-boy-racer laws and claimed he 'lost traction'. But the police didn't buy it. The CLS features traction control.

PC Mark Milton on the M54 motorway in December 2003 and winding him up in court. PC Milton was 'familiarizing himself' with his new vehicle.

Netherlands Dutch police have probably the least practical patrol car on the planet – an Opel Speedster (top speed 151mph), a two-seater convertible. Sure it's fast, but most important it's sexy.

Bulgaria Rather than sell a confiscated white Porsche 911 convertible, Bulgarian police decided to put it to good use. So they painted the doors blue, wrote 'Police' on the side and started chasing villains.

Germany Not content with a standard Porsche 911 for policing the autobahns, the German Federal Traffic Ministry signed up tuning company TechArt to create a cop-spec Carrera S. Alongside the green police markings, lights and siren, the TechArt 911 has 370bhp for a 0–60 dash of less than 4.5 seconds and a 186mph top speed.

Italy In 1962 police in Rome took delivery of a Ferrari 250GTE in a very cool shade of black. With drivers trained at the Ferrari factory, the car became famous throughout Italy. In 2004, the Italian autostrada cops surpassed themselves by blagging a Lamborghini Gallardo (top speed 197mph) to use as a patrol car. It, too, has attracted plenty of attention. In November 2004 it lost a wheel under suspicious circumstances as it left a petrol station. Can't imagine how that happened, can you?

Dressing in Drag

A 1989 Chevrolet Caprice sedan is actually the world's fastest cop car. Well, fastest-accelerating anyway. Having been retired after 107,175 miles of service with the police department in Phoenix, Arizona, the Caprice was rebuilt as a drag racer. Powered by a 502-cubic-inch engine, 'Blue by You' can run the quarter-mile in just 10.59 seconds, reaching 127mph at the finish. The flashy Italian Lamborghini Gallardo takes 13 seconds to cover the same distance.

Faking It

Speeding drivers in the Ukraine faced a new enemy in 2003 when the police introduced a prototype vehicle. The cop car was actually just a cut-out parked up by the side of the road to fool motorists into thinking they were being watched. For the cash-strapped Ukrainian cops it was cheaper than posting real officers by the road.

The Getaway

Take one good guy and one bad guy. Give them each a car, and you've got a chase.

Long-distance Runners

Australia is a big place. So it's no surprise they have some pretty big car chases. In November 2004, an Australian record was set by a couple driving a stolen BMW. Leaving a petrol station in Wirrulla on south Australia's Eyre peninsula they raced off towards Perth across the Nullarbour plain. The chase ended after some 400 miles when they ran out of petrol and were pinched.

Marathon Runners

So, 400 miles? That's nothing if you're a Ukrainian gangster. In April 2003, two armed robbers fled a bank in Wrestedt, northern Germany, with about 200,000 euros in cash and two women as hostages. They jumped into a waiting silver Seat Ibiza and roared off. The chase that followed lasted two days as the robbers zigzagged through Poland, Germany and Ukraine, covering an astonishing 600 miles. The chase involved police helicopters and up to 20 police cars at speeds of up to 100mph. One hostage escaped at a petrol station and the other was released without harm when the pursuit finally ended in Rivne in the western Ukraine. Police had held back, waiting for the car to run out of fuel, but it took rather longer than expected. Must have been a diesel.

Bronco Slo-mo

The most watched car chase in the world was transmitted live on 17 June 1994 when O. J. Simpson failed to turn himself in after the murder of his ex-wife and her friend Ronald Goldman five days earlier. At 6.45 p.m., Simpson's 1993 white Ford Bronco was spotted going north on Interstate 405 by a patrolman. The driver, Simpson's friend Al Cowlings, said Simpson had a gun to his head. The officer retreated to a safe distance and a very slow pursuit ensued. Over the next hour Cowlings and Simpson drove around Los Angeles, filmed by up to a dozen news helicopters and watched by some 95 million people in the USA alone.

End of the Road

Car chases, be they O. J.-slow or super speedy, could become a thing of the past if police around the globe take up a James Bond-style tracker dart trialled by the Los Angeles Police Department in 2005. Instead of pursuing baddies, the cops just fire a gluey blob at their car using a paintball-type gun. Inside the blob is a GPS tag that allows police to follow every inch of the car's movement from a safe distance. The device, called StarChase, could put an end to the estimated 100,000 chases every year in the USA alone. So for the cops it'll be back to watching repeats of *Starsky and Hutch* for excitement.

SEVEN

Wacky Racers

Controversy, intrigue, death and drama. The average motor-racing season has got it all. And so have we in our look at the more unusual events, most incompetent drivers, sneakiest teams and strangest stories that the sport has to offer. Gentlemen (and ladies), start your engines!

Burning Rubbers

Money is everything in Formula One (F1). The richest teams always score the most points so corporate sponsorship is critical, and racing cars have become high-speed advertising hoardings. In among the numerous cigarette brands and computer companies there have been some oddities, though, as our list shows.

Condoms Between 1976 and 1978 Durex sponsored the Surtees team as they burned rubber on the world's circuits.

Shoes The Andrea Moda team that managed to field just one of its two cars in just one of the 12 races they entered in 1992 was owned by Andrea Sassetti, an Italian shoemaker. Unsurprisingly, they were booted out of F1 that same season.

Fridges 1973's Lec March team was owned by David Purley, heir to Britain's biggest refrigerator family. Purley, a former member of the Paras, won a George Medal for bravery – not during his army career, but on the race-track – for pulling fellow driver Roger Williamson

Surtees burned rubber from 1976 to 1978 with sponsorship from the Durex condom company.

from his burning car during the 1973 Dutch Grand Prix. Purley himself survived a huge crash at the 1977 British Grand Prix and then took up stunt flying, which finally finished him off in 1985.

Organized Crime In 1992, Gérard Larrousse had a shady partnership with a company called the Comstock Group, owned by a German 'businessman', Rainer Walldorf. Walldorf, it turned out, was in fact called Klaus Walz and was wanted by Interpol in connection with four murders.

The CIA The Shadow F1 team was formed in 1977 by American Don Nichols and his Advanced Vehicle Systems Inc. The Shadow logo featured a cloaked man in a hat hiding his face (similar to the 'Spy vs. Spy' comic strip in *Mad* magazine). It was chosen for good reason. Nichols used to work for the CIA in Japan.

The World's Most Wanted Man In 1979 an unusual name appeared on the side of the mainly Saudi Airlines-sponsored Williams FW07. The name was Bin Laden. Long before Osama took up arms against the imperialist West, his uncle ran a successful construction firm and generously supported Frank Williams's efforts. This side of the family has never been connected with terrorist activity.

Xena Warrior Princess In 1997 Tyrell was struggling for survival. Shortly before the final death-blow, its cars appeared at the British Grand Prix sporting Xena Warrior Princess on the sides. Xena's fighting spirit didn't help much – the cars finished 17th and 19th.

Formula None

Getting a good start off the grid is one of the key skills every Grand Prix (GP) driver must master. Some, though, never did, because in the whole of their careers they didn't actually make it on to the starting grid in the first place. Here is Formula None's top-ten DNQs (Did Not Qualify):

1　**Claudio Langes DNQ 14/14**
　　Italian Langes failed to qualify a record 14 times out of 14 in 1990. He was driving a EuroBrun, so it's hardly surprising.

2　**Pedro Chaves DNQ 13/13**
　　Portugal's Chaves almost equalled Langes' best with 13 failures to reach the grid in 13 tries in 1991 at the wheel of his slothful Coloni. It clearly wasn't all his fault as Chaves went on to prove himself by becoming Portuguese Rally champion three times.

3　**Volker Weidler DNQ 10/10**
　　A former German Formula Three (F3) champion, Weidler didn't handle the promotion to F1 with such skill. Driving for Rial in

*1989, he entered ten races and failed to qualify for any of them.
Weidler had a bit more success when he moved to Japan to race
F3000 and even had a win in World Sports Cars before retiring
in 1992.*

4 Perry McCarthy DNQ 8/8
*Cockney McCarthy really, really wanted to be a Formula One
driver and joined Andrea Moda in 1992. But in his eight visits to
Grand Prix circuits he never made it to the start. McCarthy went
on to have a successful Sports Car career and also served time
as the* Top Gear *TV programme's test driver, the Stig, before he
made the mistake of telling people about it. Whereupon the telly
boys killed his* alter ego *by firing him off an aircraft carrier.*

5= David Kennedy DNQ 7/7
*Irishman Kennedy was a former Formula Ford star before getting
his dream drive for Shadow in 1980, where he failed to qualify
seven times in seven attempts. After the débâcle he had a
lengthy career in Sports Cars and Touring Cars before moving
into driver management.*

5= Joachim Winkelhock DNQ 7/7
*Smokin' Jo Winkelhock certainly didn't earn his moniker in
Formula One. In his 1989 season with AGS, Winkelhock matched
Kennedy's run of seven straight failures to get on the grid.
Getting into Touring Cars was a good move, though, and he
redeemed himself by winning championships in Britain and
at home in Germany.*

7 Enrico Bertaggia DNQ 6/6
*Bertaggia was Italy's F3 champion of 1987, but his 1989 F1
début was a disaster. Driving for Coloni, he had six tries at
getting on to the grid, but they all failed. Undeterred he signed
up for Andrea Moda in 1992 but his two entries were withdrawn.*

Since then he's raced pretty much anything and everything but his trophy cabinet hasn't grown.

8= Giovanna Amati DNQ 3/3
Italian Amati is one of the handful of women who have tried (and failed) to make their names in Formula One. With three visits to Grand Prix circuits in 1992, where she went home before the race began, her career with Brabham was brief to say the least. Amati went on to race Sports Cars with reasonable success and also carved out a career in the media.

8= Alberto Colombo DNQ 3/3
Another Italian F3 champ, Colombo failed to become a Grand Prix legend. After three races (two for ATS and one for Merzario) in 1978 he had a 100 per cent record of failing to qualify. He followed F1 with a couple of seasons of F2 back home before starting his own Sanremo race team.

10 Pierre-Henri Raphanel DNQ 15/16
Raphanel was France's national Kart champion at the age of 20 and is unique in this list in actually qualifying for one of his 16 races for Larousse, Coloni and Rial during 1988–9. Don't worry, he retired after just 19 laps of the 1989 Monaco Grand Prix. He followed this short stint in F1 with a variety of drives in Sports Cars, Super Tourers and GTs.

One of our Champions is Missing

Argentinian Juan Manuel Fangio, possibly the greatest racing driver of all time, won the Cuban Grand Prix of 1957. A year later he was in pole position, but would not make the start in his Maserati because of one of the most bizarre events in the history of Formula One. The night before the race, members of Fidel Castro's revolutionary 26 July Movement kidnapped the five-times World Champion from his Havana

Pinched from pole position, Juan Manuel Fangio was kidnapped by Cuban revolutionaries in 1958.

hotel to generate publicity for their cause. It certainly worked – the story was front-page news all over the world. Far from being upset by the incident, Fangio sympathized with his captors and long after the events remained friends with them.

Fast Women

Only two women have ever actually raced in Formula One. Born in Italy in 1926, Maria Teresa de Filippis drove a Maserati 250F in the 1958 season. She came tenth in the 1958 Belgian Grand Prix, retired in the Portuguese and Italian GPs and failed to qualify in the Monaco GP. In 1959 she entered a Behra-Porsche in the Monaco GP but failed to qualify. Lella Lombardi, also born in Italy in 1926, drove for Brabham in 1974, 1975 and 1976. Lella actually competed in 13 races and scored 50 Championship points. The three other female drivers – Giovanna Amati (Brabham, 1992), Davina Galica (Surtees, 1976, and Hesketh, 1978) and Desire Wilson (Williams, 1980) – all failed to qualify.

The Best Little Car Race in Nevada

The annual Silver State Classic has one of the most unusual sponsors in motor racing – the Stardust Ranch brothel in Ely, Nevada. Prostitution is perfectly legal in Nevada and so is the yearly road race, in which drivers regularly top 200mph on the public road – US Highway 318. Cars race against the clock, aiming to hit an exact target time over the 90-mile course, and apparently anyone over 18 with a driving licence can enter. The same can't be said for the Stardust – you need to be 21.

Ari Vatanen attempts to evade car-jackers on the Paris–Dakar Rally.

Sandstormed

The Paris–Dakar Rally is one of the most dangerous long-distance races in the world today. It's not just the problems of navigating the huge dunes of Mauritania that famously saw Mark Thatcher lost for six days in 1982. It's not just the terrain and high speeds that have caused 46 drivers and riders to be killed since 1979. It's the armed robbers who target the drivers and their cars. In 1988, Ari Vatanen was leading the event when his Peugeot 405 T16 was stolen from 'parc-fermé' and held to ransom. Peugeot got the car back, but too late for the Finn to continue the race. In 1999, local raiders proved even more bold: armed with rocket-propelled grenades, the 20-strong gang attacked 50 competitors, stealing cash, documents, four cars, three trucks and a motorbike.

Bend It like Brabham

The motor-racing regulations book is huge, complicated and just begging for its rules to be bent. So it's no surprise that race engineers have been creatively interpreting these laws ever since they were first introduced. Here are five of the most ingenious ways teams have pulled a fast one:

BMC Paddy Hopkirk was leading the 1967 San Remo Rally of the Flowers until the final stage when his BMC Mini broke a driveshaft and he dropped to second spot. Fixing the car would have cost a place on the podium so, allegedly, one of the support cars was brought in to push Hopkirk's car the final 20 km on the road to the finish. The supporting Austin Ambassador shoved the Mini up to speed then dropped back at the final-time control to let Hopkirk coast to the line.

Brabham In 1978 Formula One was entering its ground-effect era. Colin Chapman's skirted Lotus was dominant until the Swedish Grand Prix when Gordon Murray's Brabham-Alfa BT46B was unveiled. At its rear was a huge fan that Brabham claimed was to aid engine cooling. In reality it worked like a reverse hovercraft, sucking the car on to the track. Niki Lauda coasted to victory and the car was immediately banned by the sport's governing body, the FIA.

Benetton Formula One bosses banned electronic traction control at the end of the 1993 season. Yet the Benettons of 1994 seemed still to be able to make great starts and out-drive all the rest in slippery conditions. Benetton denied any wrongdoing, but an FIA investigation revealed some computer software called Option 13 buried deep in the on-board computers. Benetton admitted the software was for traction control but said it was left over from the previous season and wasn't used. The FIA couldn't actually prove that Benetton had used the software and they were let off.

Toyota 1995's World Rally Championship cars were limited to around 300bhp by an air restrictor that fed their turbochargers. Well, most of them were. After the Catalunya Rally it was discovered that the Toyota Celicas had a very creative device that allowed air to bypass the restrictors, thus giving the cars up to 20 per cent more power than the competition. 'It's the most ingenious thing I have seen in 30 years of motorsport,' said FIA president Max Mosley, before banning Toyota from the sport for a year.

BAR Honda At the end of the 2005 San Marino Grand Prix, Jenson Button's BAR Honda was found to be underweight after stewards discovered a second, small, fuel tank in the car and drained it of petrol. The FIA claimed this clever device amounted to illegal ballast and banned BAR Honda from two races. BAR appealed but lost.

Lowe's Racing In qualifying for the 2006 Daytona 500 NASCAR race, Jimmie Johnson's Chevrolet Monte Carlo was found to have an illegal rear window. The clever sculpting of the window redirected the airflow over the rear of the car and his team chief, Chad Knaus, was suspended from the race. The inventive Knaus had been caught bending the rules on five previous occasions. Not that it made any difference: Johnson won the race anyway.

Grandma NASCAR

The International Motorsports Hall of Fame in Talladgea, Alabama, has tributes to the greatest drivers in history: Fangio, Ascari, Clark, Moss, Hill, Rahal, Walltrip and, of course, Louise Smith. OK, so you've never heard of her, but the only woman in the lengthy list of motorsport legends certainly earned her place. One of the first drivers in NASCAR, Smith was born in Greenville, Alabama, in 1916 and started her racing career in 1946. NASCAR was a tough sport with few safety precautions, and during her 11-year career she notched up 38 wins, 48 stitches and four metal pins in her left knee. What a gal.

Eastern Promise

Iran crowned its first ever women's racing champion in March 2005. Laleh Seddigh, a 28-year-old PhD student, campaigned for the right to race against men in the Islamic republic. She was granted permission – the first time a woman had competed against men in any sport – and duly beat them all. 'Tehran is a great place to learn how to drive,' she told the *Herald Tribune* newspaper. 'It is also a great place to have an accident.'

Supersonic Shunt

While attempting to beat the World Land Speed Record in the Black Rock Desert, Nevada, in 1996, Craig Breedlove's Spirit of America left the ground at 675mph and turned on to its side. Amazingly, the speed legend Breedlove was not seriously hurt. His car may not have been the world's fastest, but his crash certainly was.

Blind Faith

Ever sneezed on the motorway? Scary, isn't it? For those few seconds your eyes are closed and you've covered hundreds of yards. Now imagine driving at more than twice the speed for a whole mile without being able to see. That's just what Mike Newman did in October 2005 when he set the World Blind Land Speed Record. Driving a modified BMW M5 and guided with the aid of a GPS system that beeped when he veered slightly off course, Newman hit a peak speed of 178.5mph at Elvington Aerodrome near York, UK.

Crushed Nuts

If there's one race you probably don't want to win it's the 'Mutha of all Enduros' at Mountain Speedway in Pennsylvania. After 300 laps of racing, the driver who takes the chequered flag has to watch his car being crushed to the delight of the crowd. The compensation is a cheque for $5000.

On your Soap Box

A somewhat under-publicized part of motorsport, soap-box car racing has a large following in the UK. The 2001 Red Bull Soap Box Derby held at Rounday Park, Leeds, attracted 50 entries and an estimated crowd of 40,000. In the USA, the sport is huge, with a national association and a world-championship race called 'The Gravity Grand Prix' that has been running since 1936. That year a track was specially built at Derby Downs, Akron, Ohio, with three lanes, each 10 feet wide, bounded by grandstands that seat 8000 people. It is 953.9 feet from the current starting line at the top of the hill to the finish line that is spanned by a magnificent bridge where photo finishes are recorded. The slope starts at 11 per cent, easing off to a gentle 1 per cent at the end. The speed record is held by Tommy Fisher, who covered the distance in 26.30 seconds – an average speed of 24.73mph.

Ear Bleeding, Drag Racing

There are plenty of motor 'sports' that we've never understood. Tractor pulling, for example. But Decibel Drag Racing has to be the stupidest of the lot. To win, you simply have to install a massive stereo and turn it up to 11. It can hardly be called in-car entertainment, because it's not very entertaining. It is, however, ear-bleedingly loud. If you were daft enough to stand next to a Boeing 747 jet engine running at full throttle, your ears would be assailed by around 140 decibels.

Now imagine 179 decibels – inside a vehicle. It could turn your brain to soup. That happens to be the World Decibel Drag Racing record, set in 2005 by Scott Owens using no less than 52 3000-watt Pioneer amplifiers driving 13 12-inch Pioneer woofers. The sound was measured by a decibel meter inside the car with doors and windows closed. So, fortunately, for both competitors and spectators the only sound to escape is that kind of annoying 'tst, tst, tst' you get from other people's iPods on the bus.

EIGHT

'Vorsprung durch Technik'

There's no literal translation for the Audi slogan that's now part of car culture. Audi tell us that it means 'Progress through Technology'. Whatever ... We all know what it means because we've seen the TV commercials. This chapter is all about car advertising and marketing: the hits, the misses and the downright bizarre.

Foot in Mouth

You won't be shocked to discover that the world's first car-maker was also one of the first advertisers. The ad below from Daimler (translated from the original German) is perhaps the earliest example of 'knocking copy' where the car-maker has a pop at its main rival: in this case, a cow.

> *A Daimler is a handy beast*
> *It draws like an ox – you can see it here.*
> *It doesn't eat when in its stall*
> *And only drinks when work is done.*
> *It also does your threshing, sawing and pumping*
> *When money's short as often happens.*
> *It can't catch foot-and-mouth disease*
> *And play no wicked tricks on you.*
> *It won't toss you on its horn in anger*
> *Nor eat up your good corn.*
> *So buy yourself a beast like this*
> *And be equipped for good and all.*

Daimler-Motoren-Gesellschaft, 1897

Playboy Centrefold

By the 1920s, the car ads started to push the owning and driving experience, the fantasy and the dream. Imaginative car advertising took hold. Nobody did this better than Edward S. Jordan, owner of the Jordan Motor Car Company of Cleveland, Ohio. His 1923 ad for the Jordan Playboy made such an impact that it was rumoured that top Madison Avenue ad agency, Ogilvy & Mather, made all would-be ad execs learn it by heart.

Somewhere West of Laramie

*Somewhere west of Laramie there's a broncho-busting,
steer-roping girl who knows what I'm talking about.*

*She can tell what a sassy pony, that's a cross between greased
lightning and the place where it hits, can do with eleven
hundred pounds of steel and action when he's going high,
wide and handsome.*

The truth is – the Jordan Playboy was built for her.

*Built for the lass whose face is brown with the sun when
the day is done of revel and romp and race.*

She loves the cross of the wild and the tame.

*There's a savor of links about that car – of laughter and lilt
and light – a hint of old loves – and saddle and quirt. It's
a brawny thing – yet a graceful thing for the sweep o' the
avenue.*

*Step into the Playboy when the hour grows dull with things
gone dead and stale.*

*Then start for the land of real living with the spirit of the
lass who rides, lean and rangy, into the red horizon of
a Wyoming twilight.*

Organ Failure

The Ford Edsel generated more showroom traffic on its launch day on 4 September 1957, than any other car in history. Ford had set up shiny new Edsel dealerships across America and long queues formed to see 'The Newest Thing on Wheels'. The car even had its own Ford-sponsored TV show, *The Edsel Show*, a live-jazz spectacular on CBS with Bing Crosby, Frank Sinatra, Rosemary Clooney and Louis Armstrong. The stars were at the peak of their fame at the time and the show got huge ratings. Not so the car itself. It turned out to be one of the biggest and most expensive flops ever. It wasn't really that bad a car. Its engine, drive-train, suspension and interior were

Even Ford's buy-one-get-one-free offer failed to sell the Edsel.

well up to the mark for the time. The styling killed it. Well, actually not the body styling. It was the shape of the front grille. It was designed by Ford stylist Roy Brown as a tribute to the luxury cars of the 1930s. He wanted the car to be 'recognized from a block away'. He certainly achieved that. The shape of the grille was unique and it quickly became the butt of jokes of comedians across the land. Who would want to drive a car with a front grille that – to para-phrase Jeremy Clarkson – looked like a woman's front bottom? Not many in strait-laced late 1950s America. Ford hastily gave the car a face-lift, but the damage was done and the Edsel was withdrawn from sale in 1959.

Dodge Balls

What better way would there be to say an affectionate farewell to one of the last-production Detroit muscle cars than to give it Indy 500 pace-car honours? So, in 1971, four Indy-area Dodge dealers sup-plied the official pace car and its backup. Painted red, the pace car had the usual options but was fitted with manual drum brakes. Behind the wheel was Eldon Palmer, owner of Dodge dealership Palmer Dodge. His passengers were astronaut John Glenn, sports broadcaster Chris Schenkel and Indy raceway owner Tony Hulman. The parade lap was completed without incident, but at the end of the pace lap when Palmer had to turn off into the pit lane it all went pear-shaped. He missed his braking point, slammed on the brakes, knocked over a track patrolman and skidded into a temporary press grandstand filled with photojournalists – injuring 19. It was said that the traffic cone he had planned to use as his deceleration and braking point had been moved. In case you were wondering, the race was won by Al Unser Sr – and he didn't get the traditional prize of the pace car. Eldon Palmer kept it.

Big in Japan

Hollywood stars do not generally front car TV commercials in the UK and USA; it's a bit beneath them, image-wise. Ed Harris was an exception, but didn't do himself a lot of good with his best-forgotten 2002 Vauxhall Vectra commercials on British television. But Japanese TV car commercials, well, that's another thing entirely – who's going to see them, apart from the Japanese? In the 1990s, piles of cash were paid to stars happy to parody their Hollywood personas and push often oddly named Nissans, Toyotas, Subarus, Suzukis and Mazdas in weird and wacky commercials. George Clooney sold the Toyota 'Toyopet II', Sean Connery pushed Mazda, Rowan – Mr Bean – Atkinson fronted a few for Nissan, including one for a car called the Martino. Mel Gibson, Jennifer Lopez, Bruce Willis and Kevin Costner all punted the Subaru Legacy, Leonardo DiCaprio the Jeep Wagoner SUV, and Charlize Theron and Brad Pitt flogged Hondas. Talk about 'Stars and Cars' – there are loads of them on Al Soiseth's japander.com website. However, not all the stars see the funny side – lawyers for several have sent letters to Al Soiseth demanding that he take their commercials off japander.com.

Bucking Broncos, Shocking Citroëns

Nowadays when we think of 'roll-overs' we tend to think of the famous, or infamous, 'Elk' test, in which Swedish motoring journalist Robert Collin, driving the brand-new Mercedes A-Class compact, swerved to avoid an imaginary elk in the road – essentially a Swedish high-speed lane-change manoeuvre – and, very embarrassingly for Mercedes-Benz, rolled the car on to its roof, forcing the company to add extra safety features to the car. But the term 'prone to roll-overs' was in all probability first used to describe the behaviour of the Ford Bronco II SUV made from 1983 to 1989. According to the US Center for Auto Safety, a Ford inter-office memo circulated in 1986 advised that it was probably not a good idea to drive the Bronco up a very steep hill. Here are a few other hyped motors that caused owners more than a bit of grief:

1967 NSU Ro80 An early 'Vorsprung durch Technik' (NSU became part of the new Audi Group in 1969). And it really was revolutionary in every sense at the time. Its styling was elegant and aerodynamic, it boasted independent front and rear suspension, electric semi-automatic clutch, disc brakes and road-holding that set new standards. Oh, and a revolutionary Wankel rotary engine that proved to be its rapid undoing. The engine's rotor-tip seals often lasted less than a couple of thousand miles.

1970 Citroën SM (Serie Maserati) Citroën's first and last attempt at a supercar. The one and only Citroën with a Maserati engine. They are very few and very far between, cost an absolute bomb to buy and maintain, and sometimes behaved like one – the early cars were prone to set their engine bays alight. But what a specification: hydropneumatic suspension borrowed from the renowned Citroën DS, power steering, power disc brakes and that Maserati engine. One of the most beautiful cars of all time. And incredibly unreliable. Production ceased in 1972.

1971 Ford Pinto This was going to be Ford's Volkswagen Beetle. A compact family car, cheap and sold in very high volumes. The tag line was 'More car for your money'. And many buyers got a lot more than they bargained for. The company hasn't forgotten the lawsuits and the public-relations disasters that resulted from the Pinto's infamous safety flaw. If it was rear-ended it tended to explode. Not something you need in a family car.

Citroën SM owners were always prepared for the inevitable Scandinavian-forest breakdown.

The ill-fated Ford Pinto. Is it just us, or does she look just a bit worried?

1979 Oldmobile Delta 88 The tag lines were 'So much outright elegance was never so downright reasonable' and 'There's a Rocket for every pocket at your Olds dealer'. It had a V8 that could operate on four, six or all eight cylinders. It was a pioneering idea that is actually being used successfully today, but in 1979 it was way before its time. The four- and six-cylinder modes rarely worked reliably and irate owners had to use wire clippers to cut the control wires.

1984 Pontiac Fiero We don't know whether the 403 service bulletins Pontiac issued regarding the long-awaited '84 Fiero is a record, but it must be pretty high on the list. There was a recall for engine fires and its reverse gear was what you might call idiosyncratic. It would engage suddenly, not at all or very, very slowly.

Reshooting Bullitt

Mention the 1968 movie *Bullitt* to any car buff and you'll get, 'Yeah, Steve McQueen, Ford Mustang Fastback.' It's a powerful association and at the time Ford sold a lot of Fastbacks on the back of it. McQueen died of a rare form of lung cancer in 1980, but he has since returned to the screen twice in Ford TV commercials, once in 1997 to drive the new Ford Puma through the streets of San Francisco using scenes from *Bullitt* via CGI (Computer Graphics Imagery) and again in 2005 in the launch commercial for the new Ford Mustang – this time reprising the cornfield race-track scene in the 1989 movie *Field of Dreams*.

I am Invincible!

Toyota's Hilux pickup famously became known as the 'most indestructible car in the world' when our colleagues on the BBC's *Top Gear* TV programme attempted, without success, completely to trash it. A 15-year-old 190,000-miler ex-farm diesel was bought for £1000. First it was driven down 50 steep steps, then into a tree, then into the sea. It was driven through a hut and dropped from a crane. A caravan was

Invincible, eh? What you can't see is the cruise missile fast approaching from the east of this Toyota Hilux.

dropped on it. A wrecking ball was slammed into it. After each ordeal, the engine could be started and the Hilux could be driven away. In the end it was set on fire. And when it cooled down – it still started. Toyota didn't need the free promotion; by 2005 the company had already sold over 12 million of the world's most popular and now the world's most indestructible pickup. Nevertheless as a direct result of the *Top Gear* show, Toyota made a fully loaded special edition of the Hilux called the 'Invincible'.

Cognitive Success

It's a legendary TV commercial. It's a single continuous panning shot. There are no tricks, no CGI magic stuff. It lasts two minutes. It was only on the very last take that everything worked and that, almost unbelievably, was take 606. If you've ever played the children's board game Mouse Trap, or seen any of the *Wallace & Gromit* shorts, you'll know where the idea came from. The commercial we're talking about is, of course, 'Cog', the launch advert for the 2003 Honda Accord. If you haven't seen it, then it's almost impossible to describe. Suffice it to say that it's like a line of dominoes made up of parts from the car. It starts with a transmission bearing that rolls on to a synchro hub that drops off a table on to a camshaft and pulley wheel that knocks three valve stems down a sloping bonnet on to a rear-suspension link that pushes a transmission selector arm that releases a brake pedal, and so on and so on and so on … It's fascinating, magical – a ballet of the car parts. It was the opening shot of an ad campaign that cost Honda a cool 6 million quid.

Hey, Big Spender

The car companies are the world's biggest advertisers, spending an astonishing $22.7 billion among them worldwide in 2004, according to *Advertising Age*. That's over $400 per car sold. Here are the top-ten biggest spenders, and how much cheaper your new car would be if they didn't blow all their money on ads:

Company	Ad spend	Cars sold	Cost per car
1 General Motors	$3.9 billion	9 million	$433
2 Ford	$2.8 billion	6.8 million	$412
3 Toyota	$2.6 billion	7.5 million	$347
4 DaimlerChrysler	$2.4 billion	3.9 million	$615
5 Nissan	$1.8 billion	3.3 million	$545
6 Honda	$1.6 billion	3.2 million	$500
7 Volkswagen	$1.4 billion	5.1 million	$274
8 PSA Peugeot Citroën	$1 billion	3.4 million	$294
9 Renault	$850 million	1.8 million	$472
10 Hyundai	$700 million	2.3 million	$304

All figures for 2004

 Motor Mania

Bavarian Movie Werks

BMW USA hired the hottest Hollywood directors to produce its series *The Hire*, which aired on the internet between 2001 and 2005. The eight short films all starred Clive Owen as The Driver, in a variety of stories that all involved Beemers driven at silly speeds and plenty sideways. Directors included John Woo, John Frankenheimer, Ang Lee and Guy Ritchie (his missus, Madonna, appeared as the Star in his film, *Star*). The Hire won BMW numerous awards including *Wired* magazine's 'Best Excuse for Broadband' in 2001 and prompted BMW to launch its own cable-TV channel. The glorified ads are in fact quite glorious, and as a result were added to the permanent collection of the Museum of Modern Art in New York.

Tooning In

Following their success with BMW films, the German firm moved into the comic-book business by joining forces with Dark Horse comics to produce short graphic novels based on The Hire. It's not the first time car-makers have tuned into the power of cartoons, though. As early as 1931, Oldsmobile enlisted the legendary Fleischer Studios (creators of *Popeye* and *Betty Boop*) to produce *In My Merry Oldsmobile*. Animated by Jimmy Culhane, it features a villainous peeping tom who asks the heroine to go as far as she likes with him in his Oldsmobile. Very cheeky. More innocent was Ford's use of Tom and Jerry to sell the Mondeo in 2003 and Citroën tempting Tweety Pie and Sylvester to plug the Berlingo in 2005. Ford presented the green credentials of its hybrid Escape during the 2006 Superbowl commercial break with the aid of Kermit the Frog. In the ad Kermit croaks his famous song 'It's Not Easy Bein' Green', then sees the huge Ford SUV and says, 'It must be easy being green after all.' As *Muppet* fans, we're disgusted. What next, the Swedish Chef flogging Volvos?

Auntie wouldn't Allow It

We touched on product placement on the big and small screen in our Screen Machines chapter. Since its faltering, early days, getting your new motor on to a sitcom or reality show has become a mainstream form of advertising, particularly in the USA. According to Nielsen Media Research, in just six months between January and June 2005, the top-ten car-product placers got their vehicles on screen an astonishing 2636 times on regular shows – and that's not including the commercial breaks. Top of the product placers was Toyota, taking almost one-third of those slots, with Ford and Chevrolet making up the top three. Of course, you'd never get that on the BBC.

NINE

Beetlemania

We could just have easily called this chapter Mini Mania or Mustang Madness, as they're just as important as the VW in the cult of the car. In our top-ten list of iconic autos we've plumped for the Citroën 2CV, Cadillac Eldorado, Chevrolet Corvette, Dodge Charger, Fiat 500, MGB, Morris Minor, Ford Mustang, Mini and VW Beetle. They're cars that attract freakish fans, crazy collectors and strange sportsmen, and we like them. There'll be arguments, we're sure, about the cars on the list, but it's our book. So if you're the disgruntled chairman of the Austin Maestro owners' club then you can write your own bloody book. In fact, you probably already have.

Just Look at that Escargot!

André Citroën's Tin Snail is a brilliant design. Closed car, convertible, bin-the-rear-seats-and-it's-a-van, plus, of course, there's nothing better if you need to transport a crate of eggs over a ploughed field. The first prototype appeared in 1939, but was hidden at the Citroën factory when war broke out to avoid Hitler getting his hands on it. It wasn't until 1948 that the car went on sale and it carried on until 1990, with almost four million made (five million if you include the Dyane, Van and Méhari jeeps). Always remarkably capable in the corners, despite alarming body roll, the one thing the 2CV lacked was speed, for even at its peak the 602cc engine only mustered 33bhp. That doesn't stop people racing them, though, but there is a knack to it. When Berg Jr and three *Top Gear* magazine staffers took part in the 2001 2CV 24-hour race at Ireland's Mondello Park in County Kildare,

Who knew so many farmers needed so many eggs delivered across ploughed fields?

they were advised to switch off the headlights on the straights at night. Apparently the hardworking alternator would nab a couple of horsepower that they could ill afford. Despite the hazards the team finished in the top ten and won the Rookie of the Year Award. But with a car as charismatic as the 2CV, why restrict yourself to land? There's a thriving 2CV Nautiques championship where the Tin Snail body is converted to a sort of Tinned Tuna instead and taken on to the water. Fitted with turbocharged engines, these aquatic autos are probably faster in the wet stuff than the conventional car is on terra firma. One even made it across the English Channel in 1989.

The Caddy Daddy

It's very big, it's bulbous, it's got masses of chrome and it's wonderfully hideous in pink. It's the grossest example of 1950s excess and it's got the biggest tail fins ever seen. Yes sirree it's the 1959 Cadillac Eldorado convertible. One writer summed up the car as 'rock 'n roll, outer space and color TV – wrapped up in chrome and sheet metal with wide whitewall tires.' Nuff said. The top of the line Biarritz – favoured by Texans and film stars – cost a hefty $7401 and had a standard equipment list that was remarkable for the time. How about air suspension, hydramatic auto-transmission, cruise control, quad headlamps, electric door locks, power windows, automatic headlamp dimmer, air conditioning, tinted glass – and wide whitewall tyres. The fact that it wobbled round corners like jelly on wheels was never a problem. This was a car that asked, no, demanded, to be driven lazily, one hand on the wheel, the other fondling the knee of the blonde bombshell next to you on the bench seat on open roads as straight as an arrow. The car's extravagant looks were an inspiration to Cadillac's copywriters:

> The inherent dignity and grace and beauty which have become
> a hallmark of Cadillac styling take a giant stride forward for
> 1959 ... The fabulous Eldorado Biarritz brings the glamour and

zest of open-car motoring to heights of comfort, convenience and luxury never before attained. Completely equipped with air suspension, the 345-horsepower 'Q' engine and every power and convenience accessory, it affords unique motoring enjoyment in a setting of interiors unmatched for lasting luxury and beauty.

Sting in the Tail

In 2004, *Automobile* magazine named the Chevrolet Corvette Sting Ray – that's the twin rear-windowed fastback version – built from 1963 to 1967, the 'coolest car in history'. An accolade that added even more kudos to America's first 'real' sports car. Designed by the legendary Harley Earl, the fibre-glass-bodied Corvette first rolled off the GM Flint, Michigan, production line in 1953. By the end of 2003,

The Chevrolet Corvette Sting Ray is the 'coolest car in history', says Automobile *magazine. And they're probably right.*

exactly 1,302,401 'Vettes' had been produced. The fiftieth anniversary celebrations in Nashville, Tennessee, in June 2003 saw the biggest gathering of Corvettes in history. An estimated 6000 cars rolled into the city – accompanied by 50,000 or more Corvette enthusiasts. Typical of them was Bruce Forman, who saw his very first Corvette as a high-school junior working for extra cash at a car wash. Then and there he vowed to own one – one day. That one day took 40 years, till he retired at age 60 and bought the exact model he washed all those years ago – a perfectly restored 1954 car. He drove his Vette 2196 miles from Camarillo, California, to Nashville to attend the celebrations. You have to be pretty loaded to afford a classic Vette nowadays. We saw one of the 'coolest cars in history', a superbly restored and cared for 1963 Sting Ray, advertised for a cool $249,000.

Put up your Dukes

Dodge's answer to the Mustang is the only car on our list chosen purely for its star quality. And it's really only a couple of years of Charger production that count. It may have been unveiled as a show car in 1965, but it's the 1968 and 1969 cars that we're interested in. There's little to choose between them visually, but when we say that one is black and the other's bright orange you'll know where we're coming from. The Charger owes its cult status to its onscreen appearances in *Bullitt* and *The Dukes of Hazzard*. In *Bullitt*, the black '68 RT gets toasted by Steve McQueen's Mustang, but thanks to Bo and Luke's wild sideways escapes, huge leaps, blasts on the Dixie horn (and the occasional gratuitous glimpse of Daisy in the skimpiest of shorts), no man–child of the 1970s would wish to own another car. And there's big business in creating replicas of the General Lee. Smith Brothers of Washington state build Generals for a shade over $30,000 and plenty of companies offer kits to help wannabe Dukes do it themselves. A Dixie horn will cost $100, a set of pushbars $350 and a full set of confederate stickers can be yours for $275 from buildagenerallee.com. Wonder what they'd look like on a Fiat Multipla?

An Early Abarth

The diminutive Fiat 500 first saw the light of day in 1957. Affectionately called the 'Bambino', it was one of the most successful cars ever to come out of Italy. Young Italian families, keen to get off their Vespas and Lambrettas and on to and into the relative stability and comfort of four wheels, flocked to buy the 'Cinquecento'. It wasn't long before the famous Italian tuning firm of Abarth had a go at beefing up the bare-bones motor. The result was a pocket rocket, a noisy, vibrating little tyke of a car, one of the most prized of all 500s, the Abarth 500. They were raced successfully in the mid-1960s, and Hillman Imp driver Nick Brittan found himself competing against two of the Abarths in a European Championship race at Montlhéry, near Paris, in 1966. He says the Abarths were 'famous for overheating and ran with the rear engine bay lids propped up on six inch stalks. Down the straight they were quicker than the Imp, but through the turns they wobbled like a tart in a tight skirt.' The upshot was that in the chicane, 'accidentally' Nick 'bumped one of them up the bum causing the lid to jump off its stalks.' Half a lap later he saw the car parked on the grass verge. And then he 'accidentally' bumped the second Abarth up the rear, at the same spot with the same result. Nick and the Imp were first over the line. He blames what the race stewards accepted as 'racing incidents' on brake fade. The 500 ceased production in 1975 after 3.6 million of them had been sold.

B Keepers

It was the most popular British car to be sold in America. It boasts the largest single-marque owners club in the world. Its desirability was such that Henry Ford II bought the last of US MGB limited-edition roadsters. What makes this, some would say, unremarkable and mundane sports car so revered by its enthusiasts? In 1962 when the MGB was launched as a replacement for the curvy and classic MGA, few pundits predicted its longevity. But it was affordable, fast,

The teeny Fiat Abarths were not made for racing. But that didn't stop people trying.

with a top speed of 103mph, and, at 28 mpg, reasonably economical. The 1960s were also the golden age for British sports cars. The MGB was pitched against the glamorous Jaguar E-Type (XKE), Austin-Healey 3000, Lotus Elan, Sunbeam Alpine and Triumph TR4 – all more expensive. But the MGB outlived them all. It was in production for 18 years both as a roadster and as the hardtop MGB-GT. Total sales exceeded half a million. Small potatoes by most standards, but not a bad show for British Leyland, which managed to cock up pretty much everything else it touched.

A Minor Mistake

After the Second World War, Morris Motors turned down the opportunity of purchasing the rights to manufacture the Volkswagen Beetle, believing that 'it would never sell'. Doh! Instead, Morris and designer Alec Issigonis – who went on to design the Mini – came up with what the 1949 sales brochure called 'the world's supreme small car ... designed on big car lines then scaled down to make it the most economical Real Car ever to be built anywhere in the world'. That it wasn't; the VW Beetle took those honours. But the Minor went on to become an icon of practical, simple, easy-to-maintain, good-to-drive motoring. It gained an enthusiastic following in the UK and the USA. The 'Woodie' Traveller Estate version is particularly popular with the Beard and Sandals' brigade. As an example of the Minor's cult status, here's an extract from the Monster Raving Loony Alliance Party's draft manifesto as part of their transport reform:

> *The Morris Minor with an 1100 engine, but with original chrome and split windscreen, will be reintroduced on a mass-production basis. State funding of the provision of mass-produced easily-accessible vehicles which can be adapted for disabled use will give real mobility to the people, and undermine the expensive import car market. Look, if the Trabant can achieve cult status ...'*

Indeed.

Joining the Pony Club at any Price

The Ford Mustang was, of course, the original Pony Car. A smaller, more nimble machine than the hefty Muscle Cars of its day, it was a phenomenal success with more than 22,000 orders received on the first day the car was revealed at the 1964 World's Fair in New York. Over one million were sold within two years and, at the time of writing, the tally was over eight million as the Pony car entered its fifth generation. Even when the Mustang was at its lowest, when it really was 'pony', to coin a bit of rhyming slang, it sold almost 80,000 in a year (1992). And a large part of the appeal has always been the price. It's a blue-collar performance car, one that any working man can get a bit hot under his blue collar about. Even the very latest, near 500bhp incarnation, the Shelby GT500, was launched for around $40,000 in 2006. All the more amazing, then, that one sold for an astonishing $600,000 in January 2006. Of course it wasn't just any car – it was the first off the production line and was under the hammer for 'charidee' by Arizona auction house Barrett-Jackson of Scottsdale, Arizona.

Maximum Minis

Where to begin? The Mini was the first truly classless car, driven b chic celebs (Peter Sellers and Twiggy), aristocrats (Lord Lichfield) and plebs alike. Over five million were made between 1959 and 2000 before BMW brought out a new one in 2001. Amazingly, despite being bigger and pricier, it carried on happily where the original left off. Mini madness takes many forms, but mostly it's in the personalization of the car. And people go to extremes. In 1985, Andy Saunders turned

The original Pony car. And we mean that in a good – not Cockney rhyming slang – way.

BMW's new Mini wasn't quite as easy to park as the original, but it was good for a spot of mini-dipping.

a Mini into 'Claustrophobia' – the lowest road-legal car in the world at just 34.5 inches high. In 1997, Rover itself commissioned a bespoke Mini Limo from John Cooper Garages that was sold for a record $80,000, and in 2004 BMW unveiled the Mini XXL – a 6-metre stretched version with four doors, a passenger compartment with TV, DVD, telephone and … a Jacuzzi. Personalization is so much a part of Mini ownership that buyers of the current Mini can choose from no fewer than 11 different roof decals, including a chequered flag, the Stars and Stripes and even a zebra pattern. Perhaps unsurprisingly for this Brit-pop car, the Union Jack is the most popular choice, even in the USA.

Love the Bug

Funny how a car conceived by the embodiment of evil turned out to be the choice of peace-loving hippies and artists the world over. In the 1930s, Adolf Hitler wanted to create a 'people's car' – that's *Volks Wagen* in German, of course. He commissioned Ferdinand Porsche, and the Beetle was born in 1938, just before the start of the Second World War. Save for the war years, the Beetle went on to have the longest uninterrupted production run of any car: 65 years. Over 21 million were made, with production moving from Germany to Brazil and Mexico in 1978. Beetles were also built in Thailand, Indonesia, South Africa, Australia and Nigeria.

That's the facts; now for the fun. The Beetle's cheap, frugal and functional nature attracted legions of flower-power fans and the little Vee Dubs became symbols, moving protests and even works of art. American art-film maker Harrod Blank painted his 1965 Beetle to look like a beach ball, added a bumper made from a basket of plastic fruit, a blackboard and a TV on the roof. He called it 'Oh My God!' and it became the catalyst for the world-famous annual San Francisco Art Car Festival, where scores of freaky mobile canvasses (many of them VW Beetles) congregate in the city.

Flower power. Despite being conceived by Hitler, the VW Beetle has always been a hippy hit.

TEN

Flying Cars and Superhighways

We could call this the 'Believe it or not' chapter because some of the stuff we've found really does beggar belief. In this glimpse into cars of the future (as predicted in the past and present) we've got flying cars and amphibious cars – but, curiously, no cars that are cars and boats and planes. We think though that the 'next big thing' in the relentless progress of the automobile is the hydrogen fuel-cell powered car that drives itself on intelligent superhighways. 'Home, James, and don't spare the horses' takes on a whole new meaning when James is the intelligent car and the horses are under the bonnet.

Who Needs Roads? (Part One)

You are stuck in a jam. You push a button on the dash. There's a whirring noise and then a hum that speaks power. Other drivers stare in disbelief as the car moves slowly upwards. The steering wheel clunks into flying 'yoke' mode. At a height of 50 feet you switch from 'hover' to 'forward flight' and accelerate with a 'whoosh' to the 350mph cruise speed. A common fantasy. Well, it ain't such a fantasy. A practical drive 'n' fly car is off the drawing board and into a third-scale test model. It needs a take-off run so it won't rise vertically out of that traffic jam, but in all other respects it meets our personal criteria for a flying car. It's called the Sokol A400 'Advanced Flying Automobile' and it's been designed by Branko Sahr, a senior engineer at McDonnell Douglas Aerospace. The A400 is a comfortable and practical four-seat street-legal saloon on the road and a fully certified aircraft design in the air. Push a button on the dash, and wings, horizontal and vertical stabilizers and propeller, all pop out of the car body telescopically.

Meanwhile, inventor Paul Moller says his VTOL (Vertical Take-Off and Landing) computer-controlled Skycar will be easy to fly, cruising at 275mph doing 20mpg. It's not street legal as it can only taxi on the ground. As we write, Paul Moller's company, Moller International, of Davis, California, is accepting deposits for the four-seat M400 Skycar for delivery in 2008 – after Federal Aviation Administration (FAA) certification. The target price for the production version could be as low as $500,000. Skycar has been 40 years in development and has been successfully test-flown. With its jet-fighter front end and huge, ducted fans, it looks like it's jumped out of a 1950s sci-fi comic strip. Power comes from eight Moller 'Rotapower' Wankel rotary engines, putting out a total of 720bhp. Paul Moller says it's the next logical step in the evolution of the automobile.

Flyer or Failure?

There have been many attempts to take cars to the sky – but not all of them got off the ground:

Failure: 1917 Curtis Autoplane Designed and built by Glenn Curtis, the Autoplane had a lightweight-aluminium two-seat car body and bolt-on detachable wings and propeller connected to the car's engine. It looked like a First World War triplane and, had it flown, would have had a cruising speed of around 65mph.

Flyer: 1937 Waterman Arrowbile The first flying car actually to fly. It used a Studebaker engine and lots of Studebaker and Ford parts. Two levers were pulled to detach the swept-back wings. The Studebaker company saw promotional potential, bought the Waterman company and funded the building of five Arrowbiles. It flew at 110mph and did 55mph on the road. However, there was no way of meeting the target price of $3000, and the project was eventually abandoned.

Flyer: 1946 Fulton Airphibian turned the flying car concept on its head. It was basically a proper light aircraft with a detachable cabin and propeller that sat on the four-wheeled landing gear. It flew just like a light aircraft and gained full airworthiness certification from the Civil Aeronautics Administration (CAA). In the air it cruised at 120mph. On the road it just about managed 50mph.

Failure: 1947 ConvAircar Is it a car? Is it a plane? No, it's the Consolidated-Vultee ConvAircar. It was a car that clipped on to a light aircraft sans cabin. Its main claim to claim was its fuel economy in the air – 45mpg(US). It crashed on its third flight.

Flyer: 1970 Aerocar Inspired by the Fulton Airphibian, the FAA certified that Aerocar worked so well that the Ford Motor Company even considered marketing it. Uniquely, its flying kit could be folded and towed behind the car bit. The 1970s fuel crisis and the advent of cheap Japanese imported cars put paid to the idea.

And just in case you're wondering why villain Scaramaga's flying AMC Matador featured in the 1974 James Bond movie *The Man with the Golden Gun* isn't listed here, it's because it couldn't fly more than 500 metres. A radio-controlled model was used for the movie's actual flying sequences.

Who Needs Roads? (Part Two)

When terra firma looks a little crowded then why not take to the water instead?

Berg Jr once drove an amphibious 4×4 in the Thames and described the experience as 'wet'. For reasons best known to themselves, inventors have been trying to come up with a practical amphibious car since the invention of the car itself. German amphibious-car owner and archivist Rene Pohl has a list of 203 amphibious cars on his website, beginning with the 1899 Danish Magrelan Amphibium and ending with the 2005 American Terrawind Hydraspider. We're not about to list all of them here, just those that we think meet our criteria of either most interesting or completely mad. Did they sink or swim?

Sinker: Amphicar This is probably the most well-known amphibious car and the only one ever to be manufactured in volume. A total of 3878 Amphicars were built in Germany between 1961 and 1968, the majority exported to the USA. Known as the '770' because of its 70mph max speed on land and 7mph in the water, it had a 43bhp Triumph Herald engine driving the rear wheels and twin nylon propellers. It was steered by turning the front wheels.

Swimmer: Dutton 4wd S2 Commander Also known as the Amphijeep, it's the only amphibious car currently in production. Amphibious Cars Limited, based at Littlehampton, West Sussex, and owned by one Tim Dutton, has been making practical amphibious cars since 1995. A fully built, 1300cc petrol-S2 Commander cost £26,617 excluding VAT in 2005. Interested kit-car builders might care to know that DIY versions start at less than £10,000. Speed in the water is 6.3mph.

Sinker: Amphiranger This German purpose-designed and built amphibious vehicle made between 1985 and 1987 looks a bit like a Mercedes-Benz G-Wagen in the water. Its main claim to fame was its use in one of the early episodes of *Baywatch*. It was priced at $90,000, had a Ford V6 engine and part-time four-wheel drive. The front wheels acted as rudders, the propeller was retractable, and the speed in the water was a respectable 11mph.

Swimmer: Hydra Spyder Cool Amphibious Manufacturers International has come up with what we can only describe as a Muscle Car Boat. They call it the Hydra Spyder, and the prototype is fitted with a

502bhp Chevrolet V8. Wheels are retractable, drive is by marine jet, the planing hull is aluminium and the four-seat body is fibre-glass. Prices start at $155,000 for the standard 400bhp version. Max speed on land is 155mph; on water it's a very quick 55mph.

Swimmer: Gibbs Aquada In June 2004, Virgin boss Sir Richard Branson took to the sea instead of the air and drove a Gibbs Aquada amphibious sports car across the English Channel in just 100 minutes and 6 seconds – spoofing James Bond by being dressed for dinner. The three-seat Aquada behaves as a 100mph open sports car on land – in the water it tucks up its wheels and becomes a 30mph speedboat. The estimated cost in 2004 was £115,000, although this should reduce significantly if American licensees manufacture the car in volume.

Swimmer: Rinspeed Splash Built as a one-off concept car for the 2005 Geneva Motor Show by renowned Swiss fantasy custom-car-maker

The Rinspeed Splash. Sure, it'll get you across the Channel quickly, but where's the duty-free shop?

Rinspeed, the Rinspeed Splash is mind-bogglingly unique. If it were in a Bond movie, it would have been made by Q. It's the only amphibious sports car that can turn itself into a high-speed hydrofoil capable of 50mph, 'flying' 60 cm above the water – calm water only. It's quick with the foils retracted as well, planing at around 30mph. On land, the Splash gets to 60mph in just under 6 seconds and maxes at around 120mph.

Smart Cars and Smarter Roads

In this third millennium, cars are gaining intelligence by leaps and bounds. Cars that can safely drive themselves to any destination on any road anywhere regardless of weather could be just a decade away. A car that can drive itself safely at speed across the Mojave desert already exists. Nevertheless, some of the then astounding superhighway ideas of early 20th-century sci-fi writers are sure to be adopted by today's traffic planners and ever-so-clever cars.

The General's Platoon

In 1998, General Motors Intelligent Transportation Systems (ITS) program manager James Rillings introduced the idea of platoons of eight or ten vehicles driving themselves just 1 metre apart in specially automated highway lanes. He said that small networks of computers installed in vehicles and along selected roadways could closely coordinate vehicles and harmonize traffic flow, maximizing highway capacity and passenger safety. Platoons would resemble electrically coupled railroad trains, Rillings said, forming, splitting and rejoining as required. Any system malfunctions could result in minor collision damage as all the vehicles' speeds would be similar. At the time of writing, the technology for the Platoon idea is available, but it's unlikely to be implemented for a while yet – even though it could treble the capacity of existing motorways.

Eye Spy

When Percy Shaw invented the ubiquitous Cat's-eye self-cleaning road-marking stud reflector in 1935, he could never have imagined its development into a unique component in 21st-century superhighways. Bicester UK outfit, Astucia, have come up with intelligent Cat's-eye studs that can even incorporate automatic number-plate recognition (ANPR) cameras and speed detectors. The company's intelligent road studs are already being trialled on a 3-km section of Scotland's busiest motorway – the M8. They're being used for fog guidance, surface-water detection, incident detection and hazard warning. They send data to the UK's first national traffic-control centre in Glasgow and are part of the deployment of a range of advanced Intelligent Transportation Systems. Eventually the intelligent road studs could even talk to your car's traffic-information system – rapidly being incorporated into today's sat-nav devices.

Getting the Hump

If you drive across an odd-looking road hump in the UK after 2007, it'll probably be one of Dorset inventor Peter Hughes's 'electro-kinetic' road ramps. As they slow you down, and depending on the weight of the vehicle, they'll also generate between 10 and 50 kW of electricity that can be used to power traffic lights and road signs. As they're driven over, metal plates in the ramp move up and down and the movement drives a generator. The patented ramps cost £25,000 each and over 200 local authorities have expressed interest.

The Silicon Chauffeur

Cars that can safely drive themselves – at least across the Nevada desert – came a step closer in October 2005 when a very clever VW Toureg, affectionately named 'Stanley', was the first robot vehicle to complete the 132-mile course set by the US Defense Advanced

Research Projects Agency (DARPA). Kitted out by a team from Stanford University, California, with a range of gizmos including GPS, laser rangefinders, radar, inertial sensors, three video cameras and no less than seven Pentium M laptop computers, Stanley finished the $2 million challenge race in 6 hours, 54 minutes – 3 hours, 6 minutes under the race's 10-hour limit. Stanley's average speed through the obstacle-ridden and mountainous course was 19mph.

Space Invader

Car-parking space is at a premium in Japan. In Tokyo, you need to prove you've got somewhere to park before you can even buy a car. But now there's a car that can at least assist with the physical act of parking – the petrol-electric hybrid Toyota Prius. Sensors in the car measure the desired parking space, and then, if it is big enough, its sophisticated distance sensors control speed, steering, reverse and forward gears and brakes automatically to manoeuvre the car fault-lessly into place. The problem is that it's only available in Japan and requires one-and-a-half car lengths of parking space. Elsewhere in the world the system only controls the steering – for legal reasons the driver has to control speed, brakes and gears.

Speed Limit Enforcer

Not many people know that if you drive a modern-ish car that has an electronic engine-management system, it could easily be fitted with a speed-limiter device that would force you to obey speed limits. The speed-limit enforcer system was actually trialled in the Swedish town of Eslov in 1997. Radio transmitters were attached to all the 50kph speed signs on the entry roads to the town. These activated the speed-limiters of the cars entering, and de-activated them on leaving. But you can breathe easy, at least for the time being, for as we write, we can find no government plans to implement the system in the UK.

Reading the Signs

Oz boffins at Australia's National Information and Communications Technology Laboratory in Canberra have developed a system for cars that not only recognizes road signs but also checks to see if the driver has seen them. If, for example, the driver doesn't appear to have seen a STOP sign, the system sounds an alert. It's called DAS, short for Driver Assist System, and it's part of a global effort to make drivers more aware of road signs. Although it's technically possible for such a system to over-ride the driver and take control of the car, it has not been implemented – yet.

Petrol is so Passé

One day the oil will run dry. But, fortunately, boffins have been busy since long before the first oil crisis looking for alternatives to black gold.

A Nuke in the Boot

The very idea of a nuclear reactor powering a car sounds ridiculous, dangerous and totally irresponsible to us today, but in the Atomic Age of the 1950s, atomic power was all the rage. In 1958, Ford designed the world's first and only atomic-powered concept car. It was called the Nucleon and it had a very small nuclear reactor in the boot. One set of uranium fuel rods provided a range of 5000 miles. The Nucleon remained a concept. The amount of lead that would have been required to shield the passengers from the deadly radiation would have weighed at least twice as much as the car.

Roast the Pigeons

Rover built the world's first car to be powered by a gas-turbine engine in 1950. It was registered as JET1 and in 1952 it set the world's first Land Speed Record for gas-turbine-powered cars on a straight bit of autobahn in Jabbeke, Belgium, reaching the then phenomenal speed of 105mph. Rumour has it that the exhaust was so hot it had to be vented upwards, roasting low-flying pigeons in the process. Rover's last jet venture was the Rover-BRM Le Mans car, which completed the Le Mans 24-hour race in 1963, covering 2588 miles at an average speed of 107.9mph.

In 1964, after ten years of R&D, Chrysler built 50 gas-turbine-powered cars for testing by selected American drivers. The car did a very economical 15mpg and the drivers loved it. But just like the Rover JET 1, the exhaust temperature was pigeon-roastingly high, reaching 500°F (260°C).

The perfect car for roadkill recipes. The JET1's gas-turbine engine cooks as it kills.

Running like Clockwork

Leonardo da Vinci designed a clockwork-powered three-wheeler in 1478. He never built it. More than 500 years later a team of Italian designers, engineers and carpenters, commissioned by Florence's Institute and Museum of the History of Science, built a one-third scale wooden version that actually works. Just like toy 'push' or 'pull-and-go' clockwork cars the car's springs are wound up by rotating the wheels backwards. A full-scale car has been built, but, according to project director Paolo Galluzi, it's too dangerous to test drive. 'It's a very powerful machine,' he says. 'It could run into something and cause serious damage.'

All Spin, No Go

The very complicated prototype Chrysler Patriot Le Mans Sports Car was developed for the 1995 Le Mans 24-hour race in the Sports Car category. It had 500hp twin gas turbines driving twin alternators powering a 750hp electric motor. The turbines also powered an ultra-high-speed carbon-fibre flywheel–generator that stored another load of electric horses. A computer decided when the flywheel power would kick in. In theory the car was capable of 200mph plus with astonishing acceleration. Writer Evan Boberg in his book *Common Sense Not Required: Idiots Designing Cars & Hybrid Vehicles* said that the Patriot never actually worked and had to be towed in its demonstration video, in which the tow truck was edited out.

The Car that Ran on Water

BMW runs a fleet of 7-Series saloons on liquid hydrogen and Mazda has an RX8 running on compressed hydrogen. But running internal-combustion engines on non-polluting hydrogen is nothing new. As early as 1935 in Dallas, Texas, one Henry 'Dad' Garrett and his son C. H. ran an automobile on water, using a patented device to extract the hydrogen. An article from the *Dallas Morning News* dated 8 September 1935 said:

> *C. H. Garrett, Dallas inventor, gave a private demonstration Saturday of a recently patented contrivance which he said substituted water for gasoline as fuel for internal combustion engines. He said it broke up the water by electrolysis into its component gases, oxygen and hydrogen, using the highly explosive hydrogen for fuel in the motor cylinder. The working model operated a four-cylinder engine for several minutes in the demonstration, at varying speeds and with several starts and stops. Garrett said he had operated the engine continuously for more than forty-eight hours.*

Electric Dreams

When General Motors announced at the 1990 Los Angeles Auto Show that the Impact electric car would shortly become a reality, it prompted the California Air Resources Board to rule that 2 per cent of all cars sold in California in 1998 had to be ZEVs (Zero-Emission Vehicles), that is, electric. Although most car-makers knew that the electric-battery car's limited range and long charge times meant that it would have limited appeal to car buyers, all the major car-makers signed up to a ZEV memorandum of agreement with the state of California. The US-produced electric vehicles included a Chevrolet S-10 pickup, a Chrysler EPIC minivan, and a Ford Ranger pickup. Japanese car-makers came up with the Honda EV Plus, the Nissan Altra EV and the Toyota RAV-4 EV – plus a plethora of EV prototypes. The electric cars were never sold – only leased, and then mainly to fleet operators. Below you'll find a list of our favourite 'leccy cars – the ones that are charged up and rearing to go and the ones whose batteries have run flat.

It looked like a tortoise, but the EV1 went like a hare.

Discharged: The GM EV1 One of the very few electric cars made by a major manufacturer to be purpose designed from the ground up. It was a sporty-looking two-seater and zipped to 60mph in a very rapid 6.3 seconds. The top speed was electronically limited to 75mph but a special, unlimited car set a new Land Speed Record of 184mph that lasted until 1997. In 1999 the batteries were changed to the more efficient and powerful NiMH (Nickel Metal Hydride). These took the practical range from 50 to around 120 miles on a charge. The NiMh batteries could also be 80 per cent charged in 15 minutes using a special high-power charger. GM withdrew all EV1s in 2003 to concentrate on fuel-cell development.

Discharged: Ford THiNK Designed as a compact, electric, city car in Norway, tuned by Lotus, bought by Ford, launched in 2001, ditched in 2002. Total sales were around 1000 – 4000 short of Ford's target. Max speed was 56mph, range 53 miles with battery charge time six to eight hours. And still nobody knows what the name means.

Ford brought the THiNK over from Norway. Then sent it back when nobody wanted it.

Charged: G-Wiz As in gee whiz, that notorious North American expression of surprise, dismay, or enthusiasm, one that applies just as well to the designed-in-California-built-in-Bangalore G-Wiz electric car. The makers say it's the world's best-selling electric car. Well, it's certainly the smallest four-seater at just 8 feet 6 inches long. Depending on the temperature and how it's driven, it'll do up to 40 miles on an overnight charge. It has a top speed of 40mph and accelerates 'nippily' – which means it's quite a bit faster than a milk float. Actually it's only called the G-Wiz in the UK. Elsewhere it's known as the REVA. As of March 2005, 900 had been sold in India and 100 in other markets.

Charged: Eliica Designed by a bunch of students led by Hiroshi Shimuzu at Japan's Keo University, it's called the 'Eliica', short for 'Electric lithium-ion battery car', and it's said to be capable of 250mph in the right conditions. And that makes it the world's fastest road-legal electric car – ever. It's got eight wheels each with a built-in 100bhp motor and with a 0–60mph time of 4 seconds it will out-accelerate a Porsche 911 Turbo. So what's the downside? Just like all battery-powered electric cars it takes ages to charge – ten hours for the current prototypes – and it has a shortish range. Driven carefully it'll do 180 miles between plug-ins. But who would want to drive this monster carefully? Oh, if it went into production it would cost around £170,000.

Still Charging: The Smart Robotic Car They're still on the design computer and may never get off it, but it's a neat idea: two-seater electric cars that stack like supermarket trolleys and are parked at airports, railway and bus stations. Slide your credit card in the slot, tell the car your destination and glide away home. If you have no further need of it, the tiny vehicle will drive itself to the nearest stack and wait in line for its next customer. The Smart Robotic Car is a design concept conceived and developed by a team of architects and engineers from MIT (Massachusetts Institute of Technology) as part of the Smart Cities Research Group. The stackable robot car is part of a 'complete rethink of people's relationship with their cars in the ever-expanding cities of the future'.

Cell, Cell, Cell

The fuel cell, the electric-power source that's going to change the car for ever and save the world, was first discovered by Sir William Robert Grove in 1839. Apart from a few prototypes it remained a curiosity until General Electric developed it to provide electrical power for the *Apollo* and *Gemini* spacecraft in the 1960s. As we write, practically every major car-maker has a fuel-cell-powered electric car in development. Most of the prototypes look little different to the cars we drive today, but General Motors boffins and designers have come up with the most radical concepts. The GM Hy-Wire, for example, named for its combination hydrogen fuel cell and drive-by-wire technology, has all of its propulsion and control systems housed in an 11-inch-thick front-wheel drive 'skateboard' chassis. GM says the drivable prototype 'combines zero-emissions with world class fuel economy and the ability to switch bodies to meet different needs'.

Toyota's Walkman

How about personal transport with no wheels at all? The 7-foot-tall electrically powered Toyota 'i-foot' concept shown at Expo 2005 in Aichi, Japan, in March 2005, is an egg-shape single-seater that walks on two legs and bends over backwards for mounting and dismounting. It's controlled with a joystick, has a maximum speed of 0.83mph and can climb stairs. Toyota describe it as 'a wearable robotic vehicle'. Dr David Gillingwater, from the Transport Studies Group at Loughborough University, UK said, 'As always with these concept vehicles, it is difficult to see "who" they would appeal to and what their role would be in the "personal transport" marketplace.' We say, 'Hear, hear.'

Sometimes, All You Need is the Air that You Breathe

Some say it sounds like a Citroën 2CV running on nitro. Others liken it to an industrial sewing machine, a lawn mower, or one of those tyre pumps that plug into a car's cigarette lighter. What is it? It's the MDI MiniCat, a car that runs on air – compressed air. The car's inventor, French engineer Guy Negre, reckons his lightweight fibreglass city runabout will travel up to 120 miles on a full tank. The car's air tank can be re-pressurized in three to four hours if you use the onboard electric compressor – which you plug into a domestic electricity supply, just like a battery-powered electric car. Or, if you're a keep-fit enthusiast, you could pump air instead of pumping iron. A 20-minute workout might take the car a mile or two. Moteur Development International (MDI) has been set up by M Negre, not to manufacture the air-car, but to sell tooled-up and complete 4000 square-metre factories, employing 120 people and able to produce 4000 air-cars a year. Financiers call it 'risk-transfer'.

Addicted to Oil

One-time oil-man President Bush pleased the eco-warriors and greenies in his 2006 State of the Union address when he said that America was addicted to oil and must rely on technology to reduce oil imports from unstable regimes. So if we're going to go cold turkey what are the alternatives?

Hydrogen

Great stuff, hydrogen. It's the H_2 in H_2O (water). It'll generate electrical power in a fuel cell or can be burned in an internal-combustion engine. In both cases the exhaust consists of water vapour – except for a bit of nitrous oxide when it's burned. The problem is generation, distribution and storage. BMW use liquid hydrogen to fill high-pressure vacuum-flask-style fuel tanks in their test fleet of 7-Series saloons, and Mazda run a few RX-8s on compressed hydrogen in tanks that fill the boot. Most hydrogen is currently extracted from fossil fuels and the extraction process itself consumes energy and produces greenhouse gases. All the major oil companies are currently researching hydrogen production and distribution, even the idea of producing hydrogen directly at your local fuel station by electrolysis from the electricity supply in combination with windmills and solar panels on the roof.

Provided that it can be produced economically in high volume, hydrogen is the fuel that promises to meet all our transportation needs. Although it wasn't mentioned by President Bush in his 2006 address, the USA began a worldwide hydrogen-economy initiative in 2003 called the International Partnership for the Hydrogen Economy (IPHE). The members include the USA, EU, Russia, China, Brazil, Iceland and India. Iceland has a virtually unlimited supply of geothermal energy from its hot springs and geysers and already harnesses the hot water and steam to produce electricity. The Icelandic government plans to turn the country into a full hydrogen economy within 50 years, while India has set itself an ambitious target to have one million hydrogen-powered vehicles on its roads by 2020. India's National Hydrogen Energy Road Map highlights hydrogen production based on steam methane reformation, coal gasification, nuclear energy, biomass, biological and renewable energy methods. Nuclear energy? Oh, yes. Masses of electricity, no greenhouse gases – in fact if just one modern nuclear-power station were dedicated to producing hydrogen by electrolysis, it would, according to some experts, provide enough of the gas to fuel every car in the UK.

Bio-fuels

Ethanol, an alcohol fermented from plants, can be used in virtually all petrol engines. It's a great fuel, has more energy in it than petroleum and is carbon-neutral (that is the carbon produced when it's burned is absorbed by the next generation of plants used to make it). In Brazil, ethanol is produced from sugar cane and currently over 50 per cent of the country's new cars can run on it. Sweden plans to eliminate its dependence on fossil fuels, replacing them with bio-fuels by 2020. Diesel engines too run quite happily on bio-diesel fuel made from a variety of plants. In fact, Rudolf Diesel's original 1897 diesel engine was designed to run on peanut or sunflower oil. In the UK a few enterprising drivers even ran their diesels on used fish and chip frying oil. It worked for a while – until it gummed up the fuel injectors. Another drawback was that the exhaust smelled strongly of fish and chips.

And finally ...

Honey, I Shrunk the Car

Another Rinspeed oddity is the Presto, a concept car that is able to reduce or increase its length at the push of a button. For city use it's a two-seat chunky-looking convertible under 3 metres long. For the open road push the long-car button and it smoothly extends to become a 3.74-metre-long four-seater.

A Wee Fishy Story

You could say it's a fish out of water, because the Mercedes-Benz Bionic concept-car designers took their inspiration from nature and the way the body shapes of fish have evolved in order to swim efficiently. The result was a shape designed to mirror the streamlined features of the tropical boxfish.

Even more 'bionic' is the use of the urea-based 'Adblue'-injected additive that reduces nasty nitrous oxides in Mercedes-Benz diesel engines by up to 80 per cent. (Urea or extract of 'wee' was first discovered in human urine in 1773 by a French chemist, one H. M. Rouelle – we thought you'd like to know that.)

A Merc that looks like a fish and runs on urea. They're taking the piss.

Motor Mania

Picture Credits

BBC Worldwide would like to thank the following individuals and organizations for providing photographs and for permission to reproduce copyright material. While every effort has been made to trace and acknowledge copyright holders, we would like to apologize should there be any errors or omissions.

Page 2 Johan Visschedijk (1000aircraftphotos.com); 11 A Little White Wedding Chapel; 15 Winnebago Industries; 23 Corbis; 27 James Mann; 42 Ben Wright (benwrightphotography.co.uk)/BBC *Top Gear* magazine; 46 Ronald C. Saari; 49 Nik Berg; 55 DaimlerChrysler; 58 Tramontana; 60 DaimlerChrysler; 89 Empics; 92 LAT Photographic; 95 Bill Milbrodt; 112 Caterham Cars; 115 George Barris; 122 James Mann; 126 Ford; 130 DaimlerChrysler; 135 LAT Photographic; 141 Peugeot; 155 BBC *Top Gear* magazine; 162 General Motors; 167 Ford; 168 (both) Mini; 175 Rinspeed; 180 LAT Photographic; 184 Ford; 189 DaimlerChrysler; 190 Ford

Special thanks to Giles Chapman for supplying images on the following pages: 28, 35, 38, 66, 69, 72, 74, 84, 91, 102, 109, 124, 139, 149, 153 (both), 160, 165, 167, 170 and 183.

Cover images *Main image, front and back:* Bugatti Veyron (BBC *Top Gear* magazine). *Top row, left to right:* Mercedes-Benz Bionic concept car (DaimlerChrysler); Ferrari badge; Mercedes-Benz Smart (DaimlerChrysler); model Mercedes-Benz (Giles Chapman Library). *Bottom row, left to right:* Lotus Seven from *The Prisoner* (Caterham Cars); diamond-studded wheel (Asanti Wheels); Rinspeed Splash (Rinspeed); Mini XXL (Mini)

Opposite *Despite appearances, these aren't early rubber-neckers enjoying the first bank holiday traffic jam – this is a 1912 Ford publicity shot for the Model T.*

The Authors

Ivan Berg has been data editor of BBC *Top Gear* magazine since its launch in 1993 and knows almost everything there is to know about cars. He has written on motoring and technology for BBC *Top Gear* magazine, the *London Evening Standard* and *In Front Magazine*. He wrote, produced and presented the *Top Gear Full Metal Racket* tapes and in the 1960s penned Britain's only motor racing television drama series, *The Chequered Flag*. He is the author of several motoring books, including *The Guinness World Car Record*, and the creator of Revs Ransome, the 1960s strip-cartoon hero of *TV Express*.

Nik Berg is Ivan's son. He's a motoring writer, editorial consultant and occasional television presenter and pundit. He is a regular contributor to *Arena*, *Focus*, BBC *Top Gear* magazine, the *Daily Telegraph* and a wide variety of other titles as well as 4Car.co.uk. His driving exploits include piloting (slowly) the world's first ever petrol-electric hybrid rally car in the 2002 Midnight Sun to Red Sea rally, topping 200mph in a Lamborghini, tackling the world's most dangerous road in Bolivia and chasing twisters across America. He has also raced powerboats and Citroën 2CVs, survived a Destruction Derby and barrel-rolled a Chrysler PT Cruiser.